acting A to Z

KATHERINE MAYFIELD has performed for over twenty years on stages across the country and in film, television, and theater in New York City. Her favorite roles have included Annie Sullivan in *The Miracle Worker,* Rosalind in *As You Like It,* and Lucy in *You're a Good Man, Charlie Brown.* She has also appeared numerous times on the soap opera *Guiding Light.*

REVISED 2ND EDITION

acting A to Z

The Young Person's Guide
to a Stage or Screen Career

KATHERINE MAYFIELD

BACKSTAGE BOOKS
AN IMPRINT OF WATSON GUPTILL PUBLICATIONS
New York

This book is dedicated to every young actor who has a dream,

and to the playful, creative child in all of us.

First published in 1998 by Back Stage Books, an imprint of Watson-Guptill Publications,
Nielsen Business Media, a division of The Nielsen Company
770 Broadway, New York, NY 10003
www.watsonguptill.com

Editor for Back Stage Books: Maureen Lo
Book design: Meryl Sussman Levavi
Cover design: Julie Duquet/Duquet Design
Production manager: Katherine Happ

Library of Congress Cataloguing-in-Publication Data is available from the Library of
Congress.
Library of Congress Control Number: 2007923549

ISBN 978-0-8230-8797-6

acknowledgments

My deepest appreciation goes to the young actors who kindly shared their feelings, hopes, and dreams so that young actors everywhere would have a deeper understanding of acting. I wish you all the success and happiness you hope for.

Special thanks are due to Andrew Wetmore, who helped me shape the book into a user-friendly form; to Sam Rush of the Smith College Theater Department; to Stan Sherer and Jim Gipe for granting permission to use illustrations; to Elizabeth Wetmore for the use of her resume; to my parents for their support and encouragement; and to my editor, Mark Glubke, whose patient and wise counsel guided me from beginning to end.

contents

introduction

So you want to be an actor! Whether you've already done a lot of acting, or you're only starting to think about stepping into the world of show business, this book can help you. The more you read, the more you'll find out on all the things that professional actors know.

In these pages you'll see what it's *really* like to try to make your living as an actor. You'll find advice about training and guidance about how to find work, and you'll learn how to take care of yourself.

"Show business" is an accurate description of the world of the professional actor. As an actor, not only are you performing in one kind of show or another, you are also involved in and focused on the "business" aspect of your career: promoting and selling yourself as an actor, negotiating with others on several levels, and staying focused on the goals you want to achieve in your business of being an actor. This book will teach you what you need to know about the business aspects of an acting career, and it will help you learn how to promote yourself as an actor.

Several young actors shared their thoughts and feelings throughout the book in the "Talking about Acting" sections. It may help you to compare your own ideas with theirs as you consider a professional acting career.

Pursuing an acting career takes a lot of time, energy, focus, and money. It requires a lot of sacrifice, at least in the early stages of a career. So if you want to be a professional actor, you should do it because you love it more than anything else. If it makes you happy to perform, you'll be more successful than if you only want to be a star. And you'll discover there are many other ways to pursue your dream of acting without making a career of it.

However you do it, acting is fun. And whether you want to pursue a career on the stage, in film, or on television, or act simply for pleasure, I wish you lots of luck and good times!

acting: an overview

Welcome to the world of acting! Whether you have an interest in every aspect of acting or just a particular area—such as TV or film—it will help you to know as much as you can about how show business works. You've probably heard the phrase, "There's no business like show business" (from the 1946 Irving Berlin musical *Annie Get Your Gun*)—and it's true. Show business is vastly different in many ways from other professions.

If you're considering a career in acting, you'll need a lot of information to make a choice that works for you. In some ways, an acting career is just like any other career: it requires training and studying, as well as focus and determination. In other ways, it's very different. You'll be going to auditions and interviews, competing with hundreds of other actors for a role, and keeping yourself in good shape. Some people's personalities are well suited to the world of show business, and some are not. As you read through the book, you'll find information that will help you decide if an acting career is right for you.

Many actors study for several years before they set out to become professionals—that is, to find jobs and make their living as actors. And even those actors who have gone through a training program and are already in the profession spend time each week improving their skills, polishing their talent, and keeping up with new plays and events in the world of show business. Pursuing a career as an actor means excitement and new experiences, but it also means hard work and dedication.

Let's look at seven different fields in which you might find work as a professional actor.

THEATER

Live theater is the most basic and traditional way for an actor to practice his or her craft. When an actor is cast in a play, he'll usually spend four to six weeks rehearsing with the director and the other actors. Opening night is a big event, when the actors usually do the play in front of an audience for the first time. For many plays there are *previews*—that is, when the play is performed for an audience a number of times before it officially opens. This permits the actors to see how audiences will respond to their work. Previews also give actors a chance to get comfortable in front of an audience before theater critics write their reviews of the show.

Most actors first gain experience performing in the theater before they begin to learn film or commercial skills. Working in front of an audience is a basic and necessary part of an actor's training, even if he or she later moves into film or television. And some actors who become film stars still return to the stage during their careers. They believe that the stage offers a rich experience for the actor that can be missing from film work. There's nothing in the process of making a film that can compare to the thrill of performing in front of an expectant, excited live audience.

TALKING ABOUT ACTING

Do you plan to pursue a career as an actor after high school or college?

Meg, age 13: *I don't really want to be a professional actor, because it's such a competitive field. I'm not really cut out for that kind of thing. Acting is fun if you don't have to worry: "If I don't get this part, I can't pay my rent." That takes all the fun out of it.*

It's good to know exactly what you want to get out of acting. Once you know that, you can decide whether to pursue it as your profession or do some acting "on the side" while you establish another career. If you like acting because it's fun, then it will be fun for you anywhere you do it. If you don't like competing against others, then an acting career would probably be unpleasant for you. Just do some thinking about what you really want from it, and that will help you make the right decision.

New York is the major theater center in the United States. Most of the productions on Broadway are musicals. Off-Broadway theaters present more classics and new nonmusical (or "straight") comedies and dramas. Off-off-Broadway theaters offer more varied fare: works by new playwrights, performance art, and other unusual theatrical pieces. The quality of production at these theaters can vary greatly.

Broadway is the most important area for theater in the country. Over the years it has become more and more commercial, which means that the majority of the producers are trying to put on shows that will dazzle audiences and become instant hits, sometimes at the expense of focusing on theater as a moving and thought-provoking artistic experience. When these very commercial shows are created, most of the work that is done aims at giving the producer the best chance of making enormous profits. Some people believe that, as a result, the variety of productions has lessened over the years. Sometimes the quality of the show may be affected.

What the commercialism of Broadway means for the young actor is that the possibility of performing on Broadway before an actor becomes extremely successful is now highly unlikely. Many of the actors who land the best roles in professional theater have already made a name for themselves in film or television. Broadway is one of the most difficult venues for a new actor to break into.

But the quality and amount of theater produced in most other places has grown. Los Angeles and Chicago have many theater opportunities, and actors can now make at least part of their living from acting in other cities such as Chicago, Seattle, Dallas, and Miami. Even cities such as Atlanta, Minneapolis, Denver, San Francisco, and Washington, DC, offer excellent opportunities for actors.

If you're not close enough to a large city to investigate professional opportunities, there is probably a community (nonprofessional) theater near your home where you can take part in productions and try out for many different parts. In local theater, you can sharpen your skills and build up your list of credits. Many community theaters choose excellent, well-known shows and have very talented people involved in putting them on. If you plan to be a professional actor down the road, you can gain wonderful experience—and have great times—by being involved with a community theater.

FILM

Film acting is different from acting on the stage in a number of ways. Although the basic skills needed are the same, the actor's performance in a film must be more subtle, or "pulled back," in style. On the stage, an actor's gestures and expressions must be large enough to "fill the house," so that every member of the audience, even those in the last rows and top balconies, can see and hear the action. But in film acting, the camera magnifies every move the actors make, so they need to control their voices and gestures. On film, if you move your head even slightly to the side, or clench your jaw, the camera will pick up and magnify the movement. If you plan on doing any film work as an actor, you'll need to take some classes in "on-camera" performance, along with your theater and acting training.

Another major difference between working in theater and in film is that, in theater, you rehearse the entire show for a period of time and then perform it repeatedly for the run of the production. But in filming a movie, you may work on the final scenes first and then shoot the middle of the film and then do the opening scenes last. It takes a lot of concentration in film acting to remember what you did in other scenes—you must focus your attention so that you can keep your work consistent through the film.

Unlike play production, the process of making a film or commercial usually begins early in the morning. The workday is long, and actors may be acting for only fifteen or twenty minutes out of every hour. The rest of the time is spent waiting for the crew to set up scenery or lights. Actors are often asked to do the same scene over and over again with slight changes. Because of this, the film actor's concentration is different from the theater actor's: his or her focus needs to last over a longer period of time on a film shoot. As a film actor, you'll need to learn how to relax and save your energy between **takes** and then to deliver a full-energy performance on short notice.

A lot of the work a film actor does is "internal," rather than the external expression of the theater actor. Because gestures and expressions are magnified by the camera, an actor has to be able to express the character's internal life with the intensity and energy that he would normally put into amplified physical gestures and expressions on a stage. In other words, a film actor needs to "bump up the intensity" of the more internal aspects of acting, such as **subtext.** This is why it's extremely helpful for actors to have both stage and camera training—the skills that are needed are very different. Many young actors look at performances on film and think that film acting looks very easy. But that's the mark of a professional actor: working extremely hard, in great detail, to make what they're doing look easy. Film acting actually requires a very high level of skill and ability.

Take: A single scene in a film, commercial, or TV show, shot from beginning to end, is a take. When everything is ready for the shot, the stage manager holds a clapboard in front of the camera. On it is written the number of the take. He or she will say, "Take One" (or "Take Two" for the second filming of the scene, and so on), and snap shut the clapboard. The clap it makes as it is shut helps the editor match up the image on the film with the sounds on the soundtrack.

Subtext: The silent "inner monologue" an actor creates for the character, which includes thoughts, wishes, and statements of feeling. We all have a "subtext" running through our minds most of the time, and creating an interesting subtext can produce a fascinating character, because the audience wants to know what's going on in the character's head.

COMMERCIALS

Again, commercial acting is different from theater and film acting. The skills required are similar to those used in film acting, but the point of a commercial is to sell a product rather than to tell a story. It helps if you are a good salesperson as well as a good actor. Commercials usually require an intensity of positive, confident energy.

Commercials are designed to make viewers feel that, if they buy the product, they will have more fun or their lives will be better in some way. So commercials usually promote good and happy feelings, rather than the conflict and struggle on which plays and films are often based.

Commercials in particular often use very specific types of characters:

a business person, a "busy mom," a young child, etc. Commercial work can be easier to come by if your **look** falls clearly within a commercial type.

DAYTIME AND PRIME-TIME TELEVISION

Soap operas (daytime television dramas) and prime-time television shows require many of the same skills that film acting does. The major difference is that most of the stories are *serial,* or ongoing from one show to the next. That is, the story unfolds and develops over months or years as the program is broadcast. An actor needs to be able to sustain and expand his or her character over a long period of time. In this instance, consistency in character is an important skill. Regular viewers come to expect certain consistencies in character's responses to events, and the line between keeping this consistency and not letting the character get boring can be a narrow one. Most actors who work regularly in this field are very highly skilled.

As unfair as it may seem, an actor's look is extremely important in most television work. You may want to watch some **soaps** or prime-time programs to see if you think your physical appearance would fit in on those shows. Even on comedy shows, most of the actors are very attractive. Of course, their comedy skills are highly developed also. If you're interested in getting work on comedy shows, a class in **improvisation** can be helpful. (Improv classes can be loads of fun and very useful for actors in any field: learning to improv well can help an actor loosen up and drop inhibitions that might get in the way of a full artistic expression.)

It will help you to watch other actors and the roles they play so that you can see the different looks and types. Most casting directors will not cast "against type." If the role calls for a tall, muscular 32-year-old, they won't select an actor who doesn't

Look: Many casting directors and agents tend to put actors into groups based on their appearance. This leads to a practice known as *typecasting.* As the term suggests, what *type* an actor appears to be is part of what lands him or her a job. The young mom, the doctor, the tough guy—these are familiar types that actors play again and again—if they have a certain look.

Soap operas are often called **soaps**, for short. Both terms refer to daytime television dramas. The term "soap opera" first came about because manufacturers advertised laundry soap during the commercials.

In an **improvisation** (or improv), two or more actors act out a short scene without knowing how it will go. They are given a theme or situation, and they make up the dialogue and actions as they go along. Improvisation helps actors learn to be creative.

closely fit those specifications. Understanding this fact can save actors from making wasted efforts to get roles.

REGIONAL AND SUMMER THEATER

Regional and summer theaters are similar to each other because the actor usually has to move to wherever the job may be for the summer, or for the season. There are theaters in just about every region of the country, in big cities and small towns. A few of them will provide low-cost or no-cost housing when you work for them, but in many cases you'll have to find a place to stay yourself.

Regional theaters primarily employ professional actors, but occasionally they hire local actors for small roles. If there is a professional regional theater in your city or town, you might wish to call and ask if you can submit your headshot and resume (these are topics we'll discuss later on). Another possibility is to find out if they offer classes for young actors. This can lead to the possibility of becoming involved in their productions.

Many of the plays or musicals that are produced at regional and summer theaters are "classics"— shows that have been performed over and over again through the years. (See chapter T, "39 Plays to Be Familiar With"). Plays that have recently been successful on Broadway and off-Broadway are usually included in the season. And some new plays also receive their very first productions—or premieres— in these theaters.

Regional and summer theaters offer actors a chance to perform in a number of different well-crafted plays and to work in a variety of styles. They can develop their skills and talent in different ways. Actors who work in these venues have the ability to play a number of different kinds of characters and usually develop a lot of variety in their work.

Regional theater: Refers to professional theaters anywhere in the country outside of New York City. LORT (League of Resident Theaters) theaters are at the highest level of nonprofit regional theater; renowned member theaters range from the Actors Theatre of Louisville to the Yale Repertory Theatre. But there are also thousands of smaller professional companies outside of New York doing excellent work, and these companies may be more likely to take a chance on a young actor. "Regional theater" does not usually refer to community, or amateur, theater. "Amateur" theater simply means that actors are not paid professional wages but perform out of love for the art—so these productions can be just as good as those in professional theaters.

Some summer stock companies perform in outdoor theaters.

In summer theaters (also known as *summer stock*), productions are often musicals and comedies. The pace of putting productions together is *fast*: each show may have only one week to rehearse before opening. At some theaters, the shows go up in **repertory,** with a new show opening each week. Because of this, summer stock will be excellent training for you as an actor. You will learn very quickly how to put a show together and make it work. And you'll find out exactly how much concentration, energy, and work you'll need to put in as a professional actor.

> **Repertory:** At repertory theaters, several shows are chosen for the season. The actors rehearse the first show and then begin performing it in the evenings while they rehearse the second show during the day. Then the second show will be added to the evening performances. Rehearsals for the third show then begin during the day. There are plenty of stories about repertory theater actors who put on the wrong costume for the play that night, so if you find yourself working in rep, you'll want to be careful to keep track of the shows!

INDUSTRIALS

An industrial is a type of show or training film that businesses produce for their employees. Perhaps they want to train machine operators to do their work safely, so they show them a short film about safety on the job. Or a company might put together a video to welcome new employees and teach them certain guidelines they should follow. Or they may use a stage show to introduce their new products or services to their salespeople and inspire them to sell more enthusiastically.

Industrials are produced for the business world and offer information rather than simply telling a story, so an actor who pursues industrial work needs to project a businesslike image. If the world of business interests you, or if you look like a businessperson, industrials might be a good area for you to earn some of your income. While not as "glamorous" as other acting venues, income from industrials can help to support you as you build other areas of your career.

VOICEOVERS

A voiceover is a job that pays you for the use of your voice. Believe it or not, this can be a strong career choice when it comes to making a good income as an actor. For that reason, the field is extremely hard to break into. In voiceover work, the actor's voice is recorded for use on radio commercials, on television commercials in which you don't see the actor but only hear his or her voice—for instance, where animals talk or sing—and for the voices of animated characters on TV and in movies.

On most commercials, the voiceover work is done by men rather than women, but women are finding more chances to work in this field as time goes by. If you want to work in voiceovers, you'll need to have a very well-trained voice—one of the necessary tools of the actor that we will explore in the next chapter. You'll also need to prepare a cassette tape of your voice doing commercials or character voices. It's best to have this recording made by a professional. You can find out more by reading books that focus specifically on voiceover work (see chapter Z, "Zeroing in on Books").

OTHER POSSIBILITIES

There are many other ways in which actors use their talents: performing on cruise ships and at theme parks, teaching at summer theater camps, or portraying a particular character at a historical site. All these kinds of jobs require specific skills in addition to your basic acting ability. For instance, if you're playing a character at a historical site, you may not need to learn your part from a script. You'll more likely be asked to improvise on an outline, as the character, for several hours in various situations.

If you're interested in some of these other possibilities, your first step might be to find a way to talk to an actor who performs one of these jobs. You'll get a good idea of what the experience is really like.

EXPLORE!

Learn all you can about acting and the world of show business, no matter what area of acting you're interested in. Try to see how it works as a business as well as an art form—check out a theatrical newspaper like *Variety* (www.variety.com) or the *Hollywood Reporter* (www.hollywoodreporter.com), and you'll begin to see how much the world of acting revolves around business.

Go see as much theater and film as you can, and talk to actors about their experiences. If you live in or near a large city, try to arrange a tour of the backstage area of a major theater or a film studio. The more you can learn, the more successful you're likely to be as an actor.

basic tools of the actor

A cting is different from most other arts because actors use their own bodies and voices, rather than tools such as paints or instruments, to create art. Painters may create something that they "see" in their imaginations, but they use tools that are outside of themselves—canvas or paper and paint—to create the picture. A musician expresses talent, skill, and love of music through a musical instrument. So in these cases, the creation of the art form—the end result—is separate from the creator. But an actor expresses and creates art solely through the self.

Some actors make the mistake of thinking that if they don't need any other tools besides their own voices and bodies, they don't need any training—that they can just get up on a stage, and acting will come easily. But actors need just as much training as musicians or visual artists. Not only do you need to train your mind and body to respond sensitively to the demands of characterization, you need to develop physical and vocal endurance to handle the demands of performing. You'll need to learn how to analyze a script and build a character based on your analysis, and you'll need a thorough understanding of theater history and different acting styles and techniques. If you're planning to pursue acting as a professional career, you'll also need business knowledge and skills. In short, you need to be an artist, historian, athlete, orator, and businessperson all rolled into one—a far cry from just "getting up and doing it."

Let's look at some of the basic tools you'll need.

YOUR PHYSICAL TOOLS

As an actor, your physical tools will be your body and voice, so you'll need to keep them in top condition. When you're in good shape can you physically and vocally express the character traits and subtle shifts of feeling that are necessary for good acting. Some roles may also demand a certain amount of physical ability. You might play a classical role where you have to **fence,** or you might ride a horse, swim, or fight in a film.

> **Fencing:** In the historic past, gentlemen fought in wars or settled arguments by dueling with swords, or fencing. Some of Shakespeare's plays, such as *Hamlet*, include scenes in which the actors fence. In the last few decades, fencing has become popular as a sport in itself.

Exercise should be a primary objective for you. If you play a sport such as basketball or go dancing frequently, you may not need a specific exercise program. But as you get into your twenties, it will be helpful to your growth as an actor if you develop a physical program for yourself. For example, yoga, strength training, swimming, and martial arts are good choices. Strength, flexibility, and stamina are very important for an actor, because the physical demands of different characters you'll play could cover a wide range. If you are interested in working in classical theater or in film, you'll need to be strong enough to handle the demands of the work and ready to learn various physical techniques needed for the style of the piece. Experiment a little until you find a program that you enjoy, because that will help you stick to it. A program that gives you a strengthening workout and develops flexibility is best. Eating a healthy diet will also provide you with the energy and stamina you need.

Whether or not you plan an ongoing program, you need to **warm up** your body and voice before rehearsals and performances. You need to have a good supply of energy onstage and be able to keep your focus throughout a rehearsal or performance,

> **Warm up:** This is the process of exercising your body and voice so that you're relaxed and energetic when you get onstage.

and if your body and voice are warmed up, it's easier to sustain your energy and express your character in a detailed way. Some actors don't bother to warm up, and sometimes it can take the first half of the show before they're focused and primed to work. If you don't warm up your voice, you may not be heard for the first part of the show.

Actors often need the skill of fencing in performance of Shakespeare's plays.

If your role calls for a great deal of physical action, it's important to do a good warm-up.

Most actors do stretching exercises as part of their warm-up, such as the following:

◆ Bending over at the waist and letting the head and arms dangle, then curling up slowly.
◆ Stretching the arms and legs gently.
◆ Moving the head around slowly so that your neck and shoulders relax.

The purpose of the warm-up is to get blood moving more rapidly through your body, to relax the tense places, and to help you focus. You don't need a full-scale, heavy-duty exercise period. Some actors prefer to lie on the floor in a relaxed position and move their limbs gently; some prefer a more vigorous workout. Again, experiment to find out how you work best. When warming up, always remember to breathe fully and deeply, in and out.

Warming up will also make your body more flexible and get you centered in your body so that you're aware of your physicality when you're acting. When developing a character, it's often helpful to explore different postures, rhythms, and gestures that subtly express the character you're portraying. Physicality is part of good characterization, and by warming up you will give your body a chance to adapt to the physical demands you place on it.

Vocal training is as important as physical training. If your voice is not well trained, strain can result, and over a period of time, strain can cause real problems with your voice. Some performers, particularly those who work in musical theater, have had major throat and voice problems because their voices were not properly trained. If you are planning on attending a college or other advanced theater program, vocal and physical training will be included in your classes. If you are planning on studying privately with an acting teacher instead, get his or her advice on voice exercises or on seeing a vocal coach.

You'll also need to learn how to warm up your voice. You can begin by humming quietly and then working your way up to doing musical scales—sliding your voice up and down. This should not be done with tension but rather as a way to get energy into your voice and get your breathing going. Make sure that you breathe deeply from your belly, so that your voice is fully supported by your breath. Many actors also do tongue twisters, such as "Peter Piper picked a peck of pickled peppers." Doing these exercises helps the lips and tongue get warmed up. Then the words you speak will come out more clearly. Just about anyone who directs plays at your school or in your town can suggest some good voice warm-up exercises.

Your voice, as well as your body, needs to be flexible and strong. It's important to develop a wide range in your voice, so that you can create characters with different vocal styles. Some characters may speak in high voices that seem to be centered in their noses—these are called nasal voices. Others will express themselves in deeper, rounded tones that are centered in the throat and chest. The next time you work on a character, try working with different voices. Experiment with slight changes in your vocal style—using a voice that's far different from your own can create a "phony" effect.

To be able to **project** your voice in a theater

Project: As an actor you must be able to throw—or project—the sound of your voice so that you are heard even in the back rows of the theater. It doesn't simply mean that you speak louder, although that is part of the skill. Projecting does not mean yelling. It's more like taking the energy you use to speak during a conversation and magnifying it ten times to fill the space in a theater.

performance, you need all the vocal strength you can develop. Most large theaters nowadays have excellent sound systems, and actors are wired with microphones so that they can be heard better. But projecting is still a necessary skill for an actor. It would be too bad to miss getting a big part in an outdoor production of a play, for instance, because nobody could hear you. Part of being heard and understood is being able to speak clearly and use your face and body so that the physical image you create supports the meaning of the words you're speaking.

If you have a strong regional or ethnic accent, you might consider getting some speech training to eliminate it. An actor needs to be able not only to learn different regional accents for the characters he or she plays but also to remove all traces of any accent when necessary. If you have a strong Southern accent, for instance, and you're auditioning for the role of a character who lives in the Bronx, you'll have one large strike against you from the start. (If you choose to attend a university theater program, this training will probably be included.)

As you probably know already, tobacco, alcohol, and drugs are dangerous and seriously damaging to the actor's "instrument." Serious actors avoid them.

USING YOUR MIND

An understanding of people and their attitudes and beliefs is essential to an actor's grasp of character and plot. If you don't feel you have this kind of understanding, you can learn to develop it by observing people closely. Watch how different people behave, and listen to the kinds of things they say. Begin to "train your brain" to think in terms of people's motives and actions. Ask yourself why someone in a dramatic situation speaks or acts a certain way. How might that person behave in a different situation? How might *you* behave if you were in that person's place? This kind of analysis will give you "people knowledge" that will be very valuable to you as an actor.

If you've decided to go to college, think about taking one or two psychology courses. Having a knowledge of how the human mind works can help you in creating characters.

As you develop your mind in this way, and learn to create and explore different characters, it's important to trust the ideas that you come up with.

It may not turn out that every single idea you have about your character or the show will be brilliant, but many of your ideas probably will be right on target. So develop your instincts, and believe in your creative ability.

When you are learning and rehearsing a role, allow yourself to come up with lots of ideas. Then you can experiment and discard the ones that don't work. This approach is much better than deciding at the very beginning exactly how you'll do the role. You don't want to develop the character you're playing only one or two steps in one direction, and you'll want to leave room for yourself to respond to the other actors, the director, and ideas that arise during the rehearsal process. It's more exciting and skillful to be as creative as you can, and if you focus on using your mind to the fullest extent, your work will be much more creative and intriguing.

If you give your mind the freedom to pop up with unexpected ideas and possibilities, with a little practice it will do exactly that. And the more you give yourself room to be creative, the more creative you'll become. Some actors with limited or rigid ideas about how a character should be expressed cut themselves off from a new angle on the character and the show. They may even miss the deeper meaning of the script. Most theater productions and films, after all, hold a mirror up to the world and deepen our understanding of all human life. Casting directors and agents, as well as audience members, often enjoy and remember a performance that went beyond what they expected—a performance that was more interesting than most of the others they've seen.

This does not mean that you should try to be weird or unusual just to get attention. Most actors who try to get noticed by being strange are not very successful in pursuing a career. With your director's help, you'll be able to make some inventive choices about how to play the character, choices that are within the natural bounds of what the character in that script would actually do. If it helps you to feel more comfortable, you can explain to the director in a private moment that you'd like to try a lot of different ideas for the character and ask for his or her feedback. Your goal is to bring the play to life and to make the best possible version of the script unfold before the audience. You want to bring as much of the variety of human nature to the role as you can, not to be as weird as possible. With that in mind, encourage your creativity, and when your body is well trained it will express your creativity in unusual and interesting ways.

What do you want from an acting career?

Liz, age 17: *Doing what I love, and having that be my mode of living, would be the best thing in the world. And if I just happened to run into fame and fortune on the way, that's fine with me.*

This is a pretty sensible outlook. Most actors are more successful when their goal is "to be a working actor" rather than "to be a star." And being a working actor is a much more realistic goal. The odds are more in your favor.

YOUR SOUL OR SPIRIT

Most audience members go to the theater or to a film to be emotionally touched in some way: to be thrilled or excited, to be moved to tears or laughter, and to feel a bond with other people. One of the most important aspects of your work as an actor is to learn to connect with others from your inner self—your soul or spirit, or "center." By doing this, you can help others become more aware of how they take part in the experience of being human.

There are many different forms of training for this aspect of acting. Yoga and martial arts, Reiki and meditation help some people to relax and deepen their connection to their inner self on their own. Some people need a teacher. In searching for a method that works for you, you'll need to trust your instincts. If you've begun studying martial arts, and you realize that it's something you're just not attracted to, try something else instead. If meditation fascinates you, and you find yourself eager to learn about different techniques and ideas, then that's probably a good match for you. You'll just know when you've found a teacher, an idea, or a program that's right for you.

When you find something you like, investigate as many different parts of it as you can. Working on your inner self will not only increase your enjoyment of acting and your ability to act, it will help you to live a richer life as well.

career issues

N ow that you've read about the different fields in acting and the basic tools an actor needs, you may be wondering if you really want to choose acting as a career. What are the issues involved? What are the realities you'll have to deal with? Are you cut out to be an actor?

First of all, anyone can be an actor. There are many, many theaters in every part of the world, and you can always find a way to enjoy acting. However, some people are better *suited to the profession* than others are. Think about these issues for a moment:

◆ Are you extremely shy?
◆ Does it take a lot of energy for you to get up and perform in front of lots of people?
◆ Are you uncomfortable with the idea that you may try out for fifty roles before you get one?
◆ Do you dislike the possibility that you might be playing very small roles for a long time?
◆ Does it bother you that someone with less talent and personality than you may be more successful than you are?
◆ Would you have difficulty working at a career while doing something else to pay your bills for five or ten years—or longer?
◆ Is it difficult for you to "toot your own horn"?

If your answers to these questions are mostly *yes,* you need to think twice about becoming a professional actor. The world of acting is full of excitement. It is a very fast-paced, people-oriented business, and professional actors work extremely hard for the thrill of playing a role in front of a camera or a live audience, for the fun of working with others who share the same love of performing that they do. And with the enormous competition in the business, actors have to be able to promote themselves continuously and tirelessly, often for a very long time.

Although most actors pursue careers because they love acting, you need to remember that it's a *business.* You'll be expected to have training and skill, and you'll need to do all the business work that's necessary to get hired.

Many actors brush this point aside, thinking that if they can just get that first good role, everything will be easy from then on. Or that if they can just sign a contract with an agent, they won't have to worry anymore about getting work. But acting is a business like many others: there is a product—you. You are the "package" that you're selling, and you're usually the only one selling that package. And there are thousands and thousands of other actors selling their own packages. You'll need to keep up on the business side of your career, or you won't have a career at all.

Many young people who choose acting as a career choose it because they have delusions about the world of show business. They see the life of an actor, even a struggling one, as thrilling and glamorous. In fact, the media encourages this view by showing mostly positive images of actors' lives (it is an "image" business, after all). To most people, it just looks like *fun* to get up in front of an audience or a camera and "play." But that's only a small part of a professional actor's life.

We never see on TV, or in magazines, the behind-the-scenes images of actors racing from audition to audition on a dirty New York street, or living in a room not much bigger than a double bed so that rent money can be saved to put toward the next set of photos or more classes. We never really see what happens *before* an actor gets a job. Television shows and magazine interviews make it look like all actors are stars whose lives are just about perfect. But when you try to find out what an acting career is really like, you hear all about how tough it is to be an actor. The truth is somewhere in between.

When you first start out, it will probably be a very exciting time for you. You'll be getting **headshots** and creating your resume and finding out about agents and casting directors. You'll be sending out your photos and resumes, going to auditions and looking for open doors. You'll be learning as much as you can about what's happening in show business. At first, you may feel like it's more than you can handle.

Most actors soon learn not to do so much that they get tired of it after a short time. You'll have lots of time to learn all the things you need to learn, so don't do so much that you get burned out at the beginning.

> **Headshot:** An actor's headshot is an 8-by-10 black-and-white photo that normally includes his or her head and shoulders. In recent years, "three-quarter" photos have become common. These show the actor's face and body down to about the hips or knees. The headshot is usually 10 inches high and 8 inches wide (portrait style), but some actors prefer to get prints that are 8 inches high and 10 inches wide.

As you go along, you'll find that you may have to go to twenty-five or fifty auditions before you get cast in a role. When you finish that job, you might have to go to another fifty auditions before you get the next role. So you'll spend most of the first part of your career going to auditions and interviews and networking, promoting yourself, and looking for ways to get work as an actor. This pattern continues for at least five to ten years for most actors.

This is not meant to dissuade you from choosing a career in acting but rather to familiarize you with the realities so you'll know ahead of time what you're getting into, with no unhelpful delusions. Pursuing a career as an actor is not always easy and fun. For the professional actor, there are some sacrifices to be made.

THE REALITY OF ACTING PROFESSIONALLY

Many people believe that acting is very easy. All you have to do, they think, is learn the lines and the movements, then get up in front of the audience or the camera, have fun, and become famous. But there's much more to it.

We've already talked about the work you must do to have a clear, well-trained voice so everyone in the audience will be able to understand you. We've seen that you'll need to keep your body flexible so that you can express all kinds of thoughts and feelings, and there's a lot to learn about creating a character and working with a script. You'll definitely need several years of basic training as an actor. You'll also want to sharpen your skills as you go along by taking classes fairly often.

Also, you'll need to learn how to audition, how to work with a director and other actors, and how to promote yourself if you choose to pursue a career. Perhaps most important, you need to know how to deal with certain difficulties. You'll need to learn how to handle the unhappy feeling of being turned down for a part you wanted—because that will happen over and over again. You'll need to know how to keep your spirits up when you're not working on a role. You must be able to deal carefully with others in the business end of acting who may not care about what will truly benefit you.

When you hear or read about the lives of famous actors, you don't usually learn about the realities of their lives and the work they do. Here are a few things you need to know to make a clear career decision:

◆ Most acting careers require a lot of hard work, day in and day out, over a long period of time. For most actors, it takes ten years or more to achieve even a small amount of success. Even after years of effort, training, and promoting yourself, your career may not be as successful as you'd like. And it can often seem that there's no particular reason why one actor makes it and another doesn't. This can make the business seem very unfair.

◆ Although you'll enjoy the times you're rehearsing and performing, there may often be a long wait between jobs.

◆ Most agents, casting directors, directors, and producers will not be interested in you as an actor unless you've already earned some amount of success. They like to know that someone else is already interested in you before they call you in for an audition or an interview. This is why actors who land good jobs will often shortly get another, and another—sometimes several in a row. People don't seem to trust their own opinions about actors as much as they trust the opinions of others.

◆ The focus of people such as agents, casting directors, and studio executives is usually on making money rather than on helping you or creating an interesting artistic vision.

◆ You'll need to support yourself with food and shelter, and you'll also have the added expenses of pursuing an acting career—and that can cost a lot of money. An actor's photo session can cost from $300 to $1,000, and fees to join a union are close to $1,000 for the first payment (see "Money and Work," page 94 for more information). And there are all the classes to pay for and clothing and grooming expenses. For instance, you'll want a hairstyle that makes you look your best, so you'd be paying for a good haircut as often as needed, and that can add up.

◆ You may have to work with some people that you don't like very much. Television and magazines tend to glamorize famous actors, making them all look and sound wonderful. Many of them really are wonderful, but actors are human beings, after all. Some are hard to work with, some may not be helpful to their fellow actors, some will even be rude to you, and so on.

◆ The media portrays most stars as "having it all," but in reality they have problems and fears like everyone else. In fact, once an actor achieves some fame, he or she is under tremendous pressure to stay on top. There are always younger, equally talented actors moving onto the scene. Some stars have become anxious or depressed enough to start using alcohol or drugs as a way to escape the pressure—with bad results.

TALKING ABOUT ACTING

What do you think it would be like to be a star?

Wendy, age 14: *I think that the money and the ability to get almost any part you want would compensate for all of the drawbacks.*

Most stars don't get every part they want. There is still a lot of competition between stars for good roles, especially among women, because there are usually fewer female roles. The director or producer still does the casting, and there aren't enough starring roles to go around. Even if an actor becomes a star, the problems of life don't go away. He or she usually faces a new set of problems, such as finding yourself at the top and figuring out how to stay there. (Or how do you handle it if you don't?)

It's not easy to face the realities of an acting career. But it's better to know how difficult it can be before you start. A new actor in New York City will find himself competing with 75,000 or more other actors. In L.A., the number is probably twice as much. Many young actors turn a blind eye to the reality of how difficult an acting career is, only to have to face that reality much more starkly and painfully many years later. You might decide you'd rather spend your time and money doing something else that you love almost as much, or you might decide that you can deal with the problems, as many actors do, as long as you get to do what you love. You might even find the challenges exciting and energizing. The important thing is to figure out whether you can live with the realities of a professional career for a long time, and whether you think you would find it a challenge, or a drag.

The road of building your career is a long one, and you'll go more slowly than you ever thought you would. Still, you can expect to get rewards along the way. Once in a while, a director may see your work in one show and have something coming up that you're right for. He or she may then give you a call. Or you may hear from a casting director you've been sending photos and postcards and flyers to. As a result, you may get to audition for a film. You might get cast in a role you've always wanted to do, or work with a fantastic director. For actors who truly love acting more than anything else in the world, each experience can be a reward for making that uphill climb.

THE "BUSINESS" VS. THE "ART"

One of the biggest difficulties facing many actors as they begin to pursue a professional career is that while they enjoy the *art* of acting—the fun and the artistic challenge of playing various roles—they are not very interested in the *business* aspect of building a career. Yet the business aspect of acting is of major importance in creating a career. You need to have a solid acting technique and be able to present your talent at its best, but to get the job and show your talent, you have to be able to promote yourself and continue to promote yourself consistently over the long haul. (See chapter E, "Everything You'll Need," for more information on self-promotion as an actor.)

It can be difficult for some people to balance the dual aspects of "artist" and "business person," but both are necessary for a successful career. Think about whether you're comfortable promoting yourself, or "tooting your own horn." Some actors are very good at putting themselves right out there and being able to say (and believe), "I'm the best one for the job." Some are not. If you are more comfortable hanging back a bit and letting others point out what a good job you do, the self-promotion aspect of a career may be difficult for you. It's true that at some point you may get an agent, but most actors spend a good many years before that time tirelessly promoting themselves, and even if you're working with a good agent, you'll still be expected to keep promoting yourself. An agent cannot get you a job, only an audition. This is one of the aspects of acting as a professional that you need to know before you make a decision. You'll want to know exactly what you're getting into before spending a lot of your time, energy, and money.

In the major cities, there are business classes you can take that provide information and a usable structure for organizing your self-promotion. If you're moving to one of these cities to begin pursuing a career, a business class is one of the first classes you should take—it's better to start correctly at the beginning than make mistakes and waste valuable time and resources.

TALKING ABOUT ACTING

What's your favorite thing about acting?

Patrick, age 12: *I like to be the center of attention—the guy that everyone else is watching. You can get away from all the things that are happening in school and in your life, and be happy for a while.*

Most actors do enjoy the attention they receive. And getting away from your problems for a while can help you deal with stress in your life. But don't go too far with this idea, or you may begin trying to ignore your problems, hoping that they'll just go away while you're acting. This can be an easy trap for actors to fall into. If you find yourself living only for the moments you can act, you may need some help in facing what's going on in the rest of your life.

OTHER POSSIBILITIES

One suggestion you might want to consider is the idea of obtaining training in a field that is more stable and financially secure than acting. You could pursue your acting dreams on a local level, with an amateur theater group in your community, but you would have a steady income from working at a job that you also have an interest in.

In that case, you'd probably get to play more of the roles you want to play, and the chance to play bigger roles over time, because once you get known in a local theater, they'll usually call you again and again. Sometimes you can help choose plays that have roles you'd like to do. You might have more artistic control in this kind of situation. In a professional career, unless you are very well known, you'll usually have little say about the chances you'll have to play your favorite kinds of roles.

Many actors have started a local theater company with the idea of performing in plays they choose themselves. This is a good alternative to pursuing a career as a professional.

Whatever you choose to do, your life is your own to create, not anyone else's. The most important thing is to choose what makes you happy—and you're the only one who can figure out what that is. And even if you take a long time to decide about acting, that's fine. It's an important decision that you'll need to commit fiercely to, not a career to rush into.

a day in the life of
a professional actor

Born and raised in Cincinnati, Ohio, Mark graduated from the theater training program at Northwestern University in Chicago. Then he moved to New York, where he's lived for seven years. At first, he had some difficulty adjusting to life in a large city. The noise and the great numbers of people made it hard for him to focus. And he had the feeling that he had to "keep up" with everything. In the last two years, though, Mark has become more comfortable living and working in a big city.

Mark lives in Brooklyn, one of the boroughs of New York City, in a neighborhood called Park Slope. He has to spend forty minutes in the morning and in the evening riding the subway to and from Manhattan. Park Slope is quieter and somewhat less expensive than many Manhattan neighborhoods. Mark needs to live in an area that isn't too expensive because he's working part-time rather than full-time so he can pursue his acting career. Let's follow Mark around on one day in his life as an actor.

MORNING

Mark gets up around seven thirty and goes running in the park to keep his body fit, flexible, and healthy. After he showers and eats breakfast, he gets on the subway for an audition with a casting director at ten. He gets to the casting director's office a few minutes before his appointment and notices that the office is busy. There are three other actors already waiting, the phone is ringing, and an assistant is opening and sorting the mail.

Mark waits about twenty minutes to see the casting director, humming softly to warm up his voice. When his name is called, he walks into the inner office. The casting director is on the phone, but she waves him into a seat. After a few more words, she hangs up the phone and speaks briefly to Mark, asking about his training and experience. He has prepared an outline of what he'd like her to know, so he feels sure of himself as he talks (see chapter G, "Going to Interviews and Auditions"). Then the casting director gives him a script, tells him what role she'd like him to read, and makes another phone call while Mark looks at the script.

Mark's university acting training helps him to focus on the character qualities and important moments in the scene. He knows he has to make a quick choice about how to put across the character he's going to play for a few minutes there in the **casting director's** office. When the casting director gets off the phone, she tells him to go ahead. Mark reads the scene aloud for her. The casting director thanks him and says, "We'll let you know." As Mark leaves the office, he feels that the audition went well, but he knows not to expect anything from it. After a hurried brunch, Mark is off to his day job, working as a waiter for a caterer.

> A **casting director's** job is to stay abreast of the talent pool of actors and to arrange for actors who are right for a role to audition for a director or producer in the process of casting a play, commercial, or film.

AFTERNOON

Mark works for the caterer at a lunchtime meeting for business executives until three thirty, and then he rides the subway across town to a photographer's studio. There he picks up his contact sheets, which show him many small versions of photos taken of him in a recent photo session. (See "Contact Sheets," page 118). After looking them over for a few minutes, he marks a few that he thinks will be good choices for a larger final photo.

Mark then calls his voicemail and returns a call to a casting director who wants to know if he's available for extra work the next day. He stops for dinner at a health-food restaurant and gets on the subway to go uptown to audition for a role in an off-off-Broadway play.

Mark doesn't particularly like the script for this play, but he thinks the director is talented, and Mark would like to work with him. The auditions are running late, and although his appointment was for six-thirty, it's almost eight o'clock before he gets to do his **monologue.** The audition doesn't go as well as Mark wanted it to because he's tired. But he's happy he got to meet the director.

> A **monologue** is a one- or two-minute speech by a character in a play or film that is not interrupted by other characters' lines.

EVENING

On the way back to the subway, Mark picks up a copy of *Back Stage,* the New York weekly theater newspaper. While he rides the subway home, he looks through the casting notices. These are small ads published in the paper that tell him:

◆ What is being cast (play, film, commercial, and so on)
◆ What kinds of roles are available
◆ Who is casting (a theater company, a casting director, a film director)
◆ How to apply (send photo or attend audition)

When Mark gets home, he prepares three letters to send with his photo and resume in response to the ads. The casting director he spoke to that afternoon had told him to report to the movie set at seven-thirty the next morning to work as an extra. (See chapter X, "Extra Work"). He sets his alarm clock for six, so he can be on time.

As you can see, a day in the life of a professional actor is a very busy one. On other days, Mark might work with an acting coach on the monologues he prepares for his auditions. Or he might take a movement or voice class. He might go to see a friend in a show, send postcards to people in the business to keep them updated about his recent work, or go to a copy shop to get copies of his resume. Some days he works both lunch and dinner shifts for the caterer—an actor's life often requires a constant juggle to schedule work and career.

On some Saturdays he spends a lot of time waiting in line to audition for a new play. Some days he gets up at five-thirty in the morning to wait several hours to sign up for a **general audition** held at the actors' union, Actors' Equity. One morning in winter, he got up at four o'clock, hoping to claim a spot close to the front of the line for a short interview with a famous film director. But there were more than fifty actors in front of him when he got there at six, and they waited for several hours in the cold and snow—with hundreds more actors getting in line behind them—before going inside to hand their photos to an assistant. The director had decided to have his assistant collect photos rather than holding personal interviews, and Mark was very disappointed. As you can see, an actor's life can be extremely trying at times.

> A **general audition** is sometimes held by a repertory company before they cast the next season of plays so that they can meet new actors. Some of the major roles in their productions may be cast before these auditions are held, but the directors are often looking for actors to fill supporting and smaller roles.

But Mark is excited by the variety and challenge of pursuing an acting career—that's what keeps him going. He likes being on the go and keeping in contact with a lot of talented people. He is lively and friendly, and that serves him well as he pursues his dream.

EVERYONE IS DIFFERENT

Mark's roommate, John, is also an actor. But he doesn't enjoy the hard work of pursuing his career as much as Mark does. He's shy compared to Mark, and so he doesn't make friends with people as easily. The noise and the busy excitement of the city distract him. He feels more comfortable knowing ahead of time what he'll be doing for the next week. For this reason the constant changes, uncertain schedules, and hasty activities John is involved in as an actor are sometimes confusing and stressful for him.

John responds differently to promoting himself and going to auditions than Mark does. He has a hard time motivating himself to send out his photo and resume. When he has to get up early in the morning to go to an audition, he feels anxious more than excited. He doesn't especially enjoy competing, so when he gets to an audition and finds that there are four hundred other actors competing for the job, or when he has to wait in line outside for an hour in the middle of winter, he often gets frustrated and gloomy.

Both John and Mark are perfectly normal people—they're just different from each other. No one would be able to predict which of them might have success as an actor. Both of them are talented, both of them may become wonderful actors. But Mark will probably be more comfortable pursuing his career than John will, simply because he enjoys the process.

Which of these actors—Mark or John—do you identify with? Who do you feel seems more in tune with the experiences you would have as an actor? How do you think you would feel after working for several years to try and promote yourself with only a little success? If you have the same goals as Mark and John, it's important to understand yourself well enough to know whether you'll be able to face the actor's day-to-day realities.

TALKING ABOUT ACTING

What do you think it would be like to be a professional actor?

Elizabeth, age 17: *Really, really hectic—like a big roller coaster. It'd be frustrating not to have a stable job, unless you're cast in a long-running Broadway show. But that's the thrill of the chase—finding a job and doing it well, seeing it through to the production, and then going on to the next one.*

The "thrill of the chase" does appeal to a lot of actors. And it is like a roller coaster. The big difference is that when you're on a roller coaster in an amusement park, you can get off and go home. When you're pursuing a career, the ride doesn't stop. It becomes part of your day-to-day life. It can make you feel there's no time to rest. You'll need to go, go, go—but let yourself step back once in a while and take time to relax!

TWO YOUNG ACTRESSES

To get another view of the actor's life, let's follow Marla and Terry, who share a small apartment in Los Angeles. Marla, who works part-time as a secretary for a fashion designer, is always on the go. She gets anxious when she doesn't have anything to do. She's eager to go to every audition she can, even for projects that don't include a role she could play. She'll immediately start a conversation with anyone, to see if she can find out about other auditions or contact someone in the acting business. Sometimes people wish she would calm down a little, or just leave them alone.

Marla also mails her photos to everyone she possibly can, and she calls casting directors and agents every week to let them know she's available for work. And she takes acting, dance, and voice classes several afternoons a week.

Terry is less talkative and less on-the-go than Marla. Still, she pursues her career steadily. She has determination. She stays in touch with people she has met whose work she respects, but she's careful not to pester them. She chooses auditions carefully, based on whether she thinks she's right for the role—she doesn't want to waste her time, or waste others' time, by going to an audition when there's no role she could play. This is a smart choice to make, because casting directors can become annoyed at actors who keep showing up for auditions when they're not right for the roles to be cast.

Terry works hard on the material she will present in her auditions. That way she feels comfortable and confident when she auditions. She shares information with her actor friends and tries to form relationships in show business with actors and directors whose work she believes is high quality.

Terry and Marla each have their individual style of pursuing an acting career and dealing with other people. Both are talented and work hard. But Marla may quickly come to feel that it's all too much for her. She's made a habit of keeping in touch with so many people and going to so many auditions that after several years of frantic work, she may feel too burned out to pursue an acting career any longer. She may move on to another field.

An actor with Terry's steady approach, who uses her energy more carefully, would probably be able to pursue a career for a longer time. That way, she'll increase her chances of success.

Which of these actors—Marla or Terry—do you identify with? Who do you feel seems more in tune with the experiences you might have as an actor? Would you be more likely to pursue your career with steady determination or work at it so hard that you might burn out?

Before you make the decision to be an actor, it's important to think about how well your personality will blend with the day-to-day reality of an actor's life. Anyone can pursue an acting career, no matter what his or her personality is like. But one person's personality or basic nature might be more suited to an actor's lifestyle than another's. You can ask yourself some questions to help yourself begin to decide whether you'd feel comfortable living as an actor:

◆ Do you enjoy meeting people?
◆ Does being around a lot of active people give you energy?
◆ Do you like having a variety of things to do?
◆ Do you like being on the go?
◆ Are you comfortable with new and different situations?
◆ Are you flexible enough to easily flow with changes in your schedule?
◆ Do you have steady work habits? Enough to keep up with the business side of acting, which is not as interesting as the acting itself?
◆ Do you try to keep yourself healthy?
◆ Do you have a strong taste for adventure, even when it's a rigorous experience?

If you answered yes to every question, you would probably enjoy the process of pursuing an acting career.

TALKING ABOUT ACTING

What do you think it would really be like to be a professional actor?

David, age 12: *I hear all these stories that some of my favorite actors tell in interviews about how long it took them to get their big breaks, and I really get scared. But if I do end up getting a big break, hopefully, after that it'll be more fun than hard.*

Your favorite actors are right! It can take ten, fifteen, even twenty years of steady work before you can make a living entirely from acting. By the time most actors have worked on their careers long enough to call it their full-time job, they're in their late thirties or early forties. And most of them never get that "big break." Building an acting career usually just takes tremendous talent and a lot of hard work over time. Being in the right place at the right time can bring you luck, but the big break is pretty much a myth.

BEING WHO YOU ARE

There have been major stars who were actually on the shy side, such as Greta Garbo and James Dean. And just because an actor is shy doesn't mean that he or she won't be successful. But it helps to know ahead of time that it can be more difficult for an actor who is shy to pursue a career, because actors must spend a lot of time and energy meeting people and promoting themselves.

If you are shy, you might work on learning how to be more comfortable with meeting people. Push yourself a little: try starting a conversation with someone you're acquainted with that you'd like to know better. Express yourself more around other people—for example, learn to show that you are proud of your accomplishments and are able to talk about them. See how this feels for you.

If you're basically an introvert—if you enjoy quiet activities and refuel yourself best by spending time alone—pursuing an acting career may be doubly difficult for you. You might consider some other artistic pursuit such as writing. There is by no means anything wrong with being an introvert—many of the most brilliant people in history have been introverted. But an acting career involves being with people quite a lot and expending a lot of energy, and it's helpful to know yourself well enough to make a good decision as to whether an acting career would be a good match for your likes and dislikes.

Sometimes young actors are looking toward an acting career as a safe way to express their feelings. If you haven't had much of a chance to express feelings in your real life, or if people around you are not acknowledging your feelings, the idea of being an actor can be very attractive. Being a professional actor can be a way to get "permission" to express feelings, or to meet other needs that have not been met in your life, such as the need for attention or respect. But the world of show business is not in any way set up to meet these needs for actors—in fact, the experience of being a professional actor can often be degrading and humiliating because of the constant rejection. You might consider what it is that you are really looking for—and how you really hope your life will change—if you become a professional actor. If you're honest with yourself, you may gain some insight into what you truly want out of life. There are many other ways in

There are few actors who don't have fun performing in *You're a Good Man, Charlie Brown*.

life to meet emotional needs, and most of them are not nearly as difficult as pursuing a professional acting career.

You don't need to try to be someone you're not. It's better to be yourself and not think you have to act or feel a certain way to impress people. People in the acting business would rather see you as you really are than meet someone who's putting on an act. Even though acting is a business in which image and personality play a major role, people are much more impressed with someone who is honest and real than they are with a phony.

An actor's life is exciting, but it can also be difficult, as we've seen. Every time an actor goes to an audition, he or she has a good chance of being rejected. The stories of actors that magazines such as *Teen* and *People* present usually don't show the reality behind the images of glamour. Even major stars have to work hard to keep informed about which roles are available, which projects they might want to do, and what kind of image the public has of them. Our society tends to raise the big actors to a high position—that's why they're called stars, after all. Their lives are made to look easy and fun, while the effort that led to their prestige, and the problems that can go along with fame, stay hidden from the public view.

There are a lot of actors who are not household names, but you see their faces in roles here and there, in the movies, in commercials, or on TV shows. Most of these actors are happy to be working on a steady basis. They don't have to deal with the loss of privacy and some of the other problems that come with being well known.

Many actors spend years working in regional theaters (see page 7), playing several roles in one season at a theater and then moving to a new area to work with another theater. Some of these actors, like James Cromwell (*Babe, LA Confidential*) and Mercedes Ruehl (*The Fisher King, Lost in Yonkers*), move on to stardom after working in regional theater for many years. But they never forget how regional theater gave them many happy acting experiences. Some actors make the choice to stay on this level for most of their careers. And some choose to stay in cities like Chicago or Seattle, away from the hustle and bustle of New York and Los Angeles. They may make only part of their living from acting, but that is a good life to them.

The point is that you can make choices about what you want as you go along. What you expect from acting has a lot to do with those choices. Don't just let things happen to you that force you to go this way or that. Do some soul searching to discover how you want to live your life before you make a choice about a professional career. And remember that no matter what choice you make—about almost anything in your life—you can always change your mind if it's not working for you.

No one can predict who will be successful and who will not. There are very talented actors who didn't become successful, for no apparent reason at all. And some actors you see in big roles might seem to have very little talent. If you love acting more than anything else in the world, if performing makes you happier than anything else you do, then you should go ahead and pursue a career as an actor. Who knows what will happen?

But don't forget: acting is just like any other business; it takes a lot of time and effort to lay the foundation and build steadily on it in order to succeed.

everything you'll need

Now that you have a feeling for what it's like to be a professional actor, it's time to give you a list of all the things a young actor needs. First we'll discuss the skills that you'll need to develop, and then we'll cover the objects or tools you'll need, such as photos and resumes, that will help you **promote** yourself as an actor.

Promoting yourself includes sending photos and resumes to casting directors and agents and sending **flyers** about a show or film you're in to people in the business. Some actors put their photos in theatrical newspapers or on the Internet at specific casting sites to promote themselves. You can look into these possibilities and decide for yourself whether they'll help you.

You can be creative in promoting yourself, but don't let your ideas get too weird. If you have an unusual idea about promoting yourself, but aren't sure if it would work, ask for advice from a teacher or someone else that you trust. You always want what you do to look professional and businesslike.

Promotion also includes having a variety of

Promote: This term refers to the tasks actors do to increase the chances that they'll get jobs on the stage, in films, and on TV. When a business begins to sell a product, it usually promotes it through marketing and advertising. When you promote yourself as an actor, you're advertising yourself as a professional, ready to do a role.

Flyers: These are announcements, usually printed on one sheet of colored paper, of the performances of a play, the location of the theater, the dates and times of the show, and the cast. They are simple tools for promoting shows and the actors in them.

audition monologues that you've memorized and rehearsed many times so you're always ready if an audition comes up suddenly. It's best to choose your monologues from less-well-known plays so that you're not using the same monologue that a lot of other actors are using and to work on it just as much as you would for a role that you're cast in so that you do your best in auditions.

As you choose monologues, keep in mind the different kinds of auditions you might attend. You'll probably want to include both a comic monologue in your repertoire and a more dramatic piece. If you want to do classical theater, you can add a comic and dramatic monologue from classical plays. And if you're a singer, you'll want to have a couple of "up-tempo" songs and a couple of ballads. Choose pieces from roles that you could actually play at the age you are right now. Choosing a monologue for a character for which you would not be cast could make the casting person doubt your ability to see yourself clearly as an actor.

Keep in mind that you may be auditioning for some of the same people over time. This means that you'll want to continually expand your repertoire of monologues as you build your career. You might ask your acting teacher for monologue suggestions.

WORKING ON SKILLS

Some of the skills you'll need to become a professional actor include those mentioned in chapter B, "Basic Tools of the Actor." In addition, movement training or dance classes will give you a feeling of being comfortable in your body. In acting classes you'll learn to feel at ease onstage in front of people. And with vocal study, especially if your voice is quiet, you'll need some training so that you can project your voice and speak with expression.

You'll also need to learn how to memorize your lines. This is a skill that you can pick up in your own way, however you can do it best. Some people like to read their lines over and over in order to memorize them. Some study them silently without speaking them out loud. We'll say more about memorizing lines later (see chapter I, "In Rehearsal").

If you'd like to perform in musicals, you'll need the skills of singing and dancing as well. Ask for advice on finding a good singing teacher.

Some are very good, and a few are not. Do your best to study with some-one people respect. (You can ask your acting teacher, a director, or anoth-er actor who has a good voice.) For dance classes, you could start with either ballet or modern dance. You'll probably want to take some tap and jazz classes, too—the dances in most musicals are based on these styles. Ballroom dances, such as the waltz, can be good to learn because they'll add a graceful quality to your movement and sometimes are used in his-torical plays and films. If you can learn to play any musical instruments—especially piano or guitar—you'll have a few more chances to be cast in certain kinds of shows.

TALKING ABOUT ACTING

What do you think would be the hardest thing about being a professional actor?

Owen, age 13: *The stress of not getting parts has to be very difficult. It's def-initely one of those jobs that's for the brave of heart.*

You need about as much courage, stamina, and drive as an Olympic athlete. Because even if you do "win the medal" and get roles, there are always more competitions to win. You really have to want to be an actor so badly that you will give it your all for as long as it takes.

Most of the productions on Broadway today are musicals, and it's unlikely that this will change in the near future. So even if you decide you'd rather do straight theater (without music), it still might be a good idea to learn to sing and dance fairly well. Any skill that increases the range of what you can do will increase your chances of being cast.

OTHER TOOLS YOU'LL NEED

As you probably know, the actor's main tools of promotion are his or her photo and resume. The photo is an 8-by-10 black-and-white headshot. The resume, which lists the actor's experience and training, is stapled to the back of the photo. You can learn more about photos and resumes in the "Photos" and "Resumes" chapters later in the book.

You'll also need postcards—that is, a postcard-size print of one or two of your photos, with your name and voicemail or cell phone number printed at the bottom. With postcards, you can stay in contact with people in the business quickly and easily. You can let them know when you're involved in a project by sending a postcard with the info printed or written on it. This way, you don't have to send a photo and resume every time—which could get very expensive.

Both the photos and the postcards can be duplicated at a printing company that specializes in actors' photos—you can look in the yellow pages under Photographic Reproduction, or ask a photographer who specializes in actors' photos for advice. Sometimes you can get a better deal with a company that is not based in New York or L.A. by searching the Internet—a good example is ABC Pictures in Missouri, which has been supplying actors with photos and postcards for years. You can find them online at www.abcpictures.com or call them at (417) 869-3456.

As an actor, you'll be mailing your photo and resume to casting directors, agents, and possibly directors and producers—the people who cast the roles or have access to casting information. You'll make lots of trips to the post office and spend quite a bit on postage. This chapter is about *all* the things you'll need, so here are two more items every beginning actor has to pay serious attention to: writing paper and envelopes. They may not be exciting, but believe it or not, they're important! Good quality paper and envelopes will help you present a professional image.

Actors need to get a supply of 9-by-12-inch envelopes for sending photos and resumes. These are usually made of a stiff, yellowish paper. If you have a large budget to play with, you can use colored envelopes—these come in cheerful colors such as blue, green, pink, and red. Some actors like to use them because they attract a little more attention than the plain ones when they show up in someone's mail. But they are more expensive than the regular envelopes. If you do choose colored envelopes, you're probably better off picking a color that's not too extreme. If it's neon green or bright orange, you may turn some people off.

Another helpful item is a box of labels for addressing the envelopes. If you can type the names and addresses for the people you're mailing to, your envelopes will look more professional. You can also buy preprinted labels at many theatrical bookstores, or online at www.hendersonenterprises.com, among others.

You'll also need some 8½ -by-11-inch paper to type your **cover letters** on. Your name, address, and telephone number should be printed at the top (letterhead). You can have a printing company create your letterhead, or you can make it yourself if you have a computer. Choose the best quality of paper you can afford, and if there's a pale or pastel color that seems to express your "essence" as an actor, use that as well. Every part of your mailing "package" creates an image of you. Think about the image you want to project as an actor: Bold? Delicate? Girl or boy next door? The paper color and design of your letterhead can say a lot—make sure your whole package sends a consistent message.

A computer is also very handy for setting up an organizational system to keep track of where and when you send photos and postcards and any responses you receive. As you begin to build your career, you'll need a good system for keeping track of your contacts. If you don't have a computer, you can set up a system using one 3-by-5 card for each person in the business you're mailing to. This way, if you get a call out of the blue from a director or casting person to audition for a role, you'll be able to check your records and find out when or why you contacted them. If you find out that a casting office is seeking submissions for a role that is exactly right for you, you'll know whether they might have seen your photo before. The organizational process will also help you feel as if you have some control in a business in which it often feels like an actor has none at all. It's simply a way to keep yourself grounded and on track.

Here's one form you might use to set up your system. Use this idea as

Name	Sent photo	Notes (Response)	Sent postcard	Notes (Response)	Sent flyer for show	Notes (Response)
Very Fine Casting	6/16/07	Requested video—sent on 6/25/07	8/01/07 9/04/07		9/04/07	[Video still not returned—**CALL!**]
Dobey James (Agent)	6/16/07		8/01/07		9/05/07	
Kim Burrey (ABC)	6/16/07		8/01/07	Went to her workshop on 8/12/07, said to keep in touch	9/05/07	

a guide, and find your own best way to keep track of contacts. An organizational system is only good if it works for you.

As you can see, as your list of contacts grows (and the number can reach into the hundreds), it can become more and more difficult to keep track of them if you don't have a system. It's a bit embarrassing to ask someone if they'd like to see your video and have them respond, "Oh, you have a new one?" because you sent your video to them three months before. So keep track of your self-promotion efforts and activities from the start of your career.

Some kind of calendar will help you keep track of your audition appointments, rehearsals, and performances. The best kind to have is a pocket-sized one that you can carry around easily. And it should have enough room in each day's space to record several events. You might have three auditions in one day, an appointment with a photographer, and a rehearsal in the evening. Remember, you're going to be busy!

WHAT YOU'LL NEED TO READ

You can usually find listings of auditions in your area in the arts section of the local newspaper. If you live in a big city, there may be a weekly newspaper that covers only the arts. Ask at a good newsstand or at the library to find out about publications you would read as an actor. In New York, you'd read *Back Stage,* and in Los Angeles, you'd read *Back Stage West* (the listings from both newspapers can be found at www.backstage.com). If you're organized, every week you'll sit down with the newspaper and your calendar and write in the times and places of auditions you want to go to. If you're out of town, or don't have access to audition publications, you can use the online access at www.backstage.com (or search auditions at a number of other sites), but usually a membership fee is required to join.

Another good reference that you can use to research industry possibilities is *Ross Reports* (www.backstage.com/bso/rossreports/index.jsp), a listing of major television producers, TV shows, casting directors, and agents that is updated monthly. This publication offers a wealth of useful information for the actor. For instance, you can use it to find out what types of projects a particular casting director usually does—some focus on commercials, some on theater, some on film, etc. You can also find out which agents handle primarily commercial or primarily theater/film actors—this way you can focus on the areas you're most interested in. For any publication that lists agents and casting directors, make sure that you get a recent copy, because there are frequent changes in the industry, and it doesn't create a good business impression to send material to someone who no longer works at an office. Henderson Enterprises (www.hendersonenterprises.com) also offers frequently updated guides to casting directors and agents.

There are also many other things for actors to read, plenty of books on acting technique and theater and show-business magazines full of fascinating articles. You can search an Internet bookstore like Amazon.com for books on theater and acting, a local bookstore, or check out the Drama Bookshop in New York online at www.dramabookshop.com.

CLOTHING

Finally, you'll need a nice outfit or two to wear to auditions and a pair of neat, clean shoes. Actors need clothing and shoes that are comfortable. You may have to stand in line for long periods of time at auditions, and there's nothing worse than having your feet hurt or wishing you could just get out of your clothes. You want to have your mind on your acting and be relaxed and ready to do your best work—rather than thinking about how uncomfortable you are. See if you can get some professional advice about the colors and styles that look best on you. If you look and feel great, you'll not only get a good response, but you'll enjoy auditions more.

finding out about casting directors and agents

Casting directors and agents are professional show-business people who find the actors needed for plays, films, television shows, and even commercials. You will want to stay in contact with them as your career progresses.

They are certainly key people, but actors need to remember an important point: casting directors and agents do not see their job as helping actors to get their careers going. Instead, they are usually most interested in whether your look and your talent are exactly what *they* need to market you to producers and directors. If they think your skills and abilities and your look are marketable, they will do so in order to make their living.

Some beginning actors believe that if they can get to know a top casting director or sign a contract with an agent, their career will progress steadily. But this is not the case. Both casting directors and agents are usually more interested in actors who have already made at least a small name for themselves in theater, film, or commercials.

This doesn't mean it's a waste of time to mail them your photo and resume, because it helps them to remember you if you keep them informed about your performances as you build your career. It simply means that they probably won't contact you until you've had at least a small part in a film or performed in a show off-off-Broadway. Casting directors and agents see so many actors that it takes a while before they're aware of who you are. Many of them receive hundreds of photos from actors every week. In the same way that it takes you some time to find out who they are and what they might be looking for, it takes them time to remember an actor's name and face.

But there is a good reason to stay in contact with casting directors and agents. One day, if you get to where you're doing regular work and you've kept in touch, they'll already be familiar with you. At that point, if a role comes along for which you're well suited, they'll probably give you a call.

CASTING DIRECTORS

When a director of a play or film is ready to cast the roles, he or she will often hire a casting director to suggest actors for at least some of the parts. Sometimes there are parts that are difficult to cast—such as a very short, very fat actor, or a person who can speak a certain foreign language. Casting directors save directors all the work of learning about a large variety of actors. Most directors make a point of seeing new shows and getting to know actors whose work they respect. But the talent pool of actors in any major city is so large that it's impossible for a director to keep track of every actor he or she might want to consider for a part. A casting director's job is to know which actors might be particularly good for a role.

TALKING ABOUT ACTING

What do you think it would be like to be a professional actor?

Kate, age 15: *Very difficult. Trying to impress your possible employer in under three minutes is very hard.*

This is one of the major obstacles for the actor: how do you impress your would-be employer in under three minutes? Many actors attempt to do this by cramming everything they can do into one short audition, and sometimes those actors end up appearing to be "all over the place." It's much better to do one thing and do it well than to try to show everything you can do in a couple of minutes. After all, you'd like to leave them wanting more! Try choosing a single focus for your audition piece, such as one particular character trait that comes out very strongly at that moment in the character's life, or one emotional state that becomes more and more intense as the monologue progresses, or one objective (goal) that the character is really fighting for at that moment. This narrows your focus, and can make the monologue much clearer and cleaner.

The director sends the casting director a description of the characters that need to be cast. Then the casting director will call in several actors to audition before narrowing the list to just a few. Those actors will then have a **callback** to audition for the director. Casting directors are under tremendous time pressure, because they often have to complete the entire casting process in only a week or two. They may sometimes seem abrupt or rude to actors for that reason.

Callback: This term is used a great deal by actors. It means a second audition or interview for the same role. You usually audition in front of more people at the callback than you do at the first audition.

Let's say you're starting out as an actor. You want to introduce yourself to a casting director first by mail: you send him or her your photo and resume, along with your cover letter (see page 130) and a flyer for a show you're in. If you've done some film work, you can mention in your cover letter that you'd like to mail in a videotape containing clips (scenes) of your film work. (See chapter V, "Videos"). It's best not to send a video right off the bat without first asking if they will accept it. Again, casting directors are so busy that they may not have a chance to look at the tape, and it may get lost at their office. They may just throw it away if they don't know who you are, and that's a waste of money.

It's best to contact people first by mail, because most casting directors are so busy they won't like your dropping by without notice. If they've worked with you before, they might appreciate it, *maybe*, but generally they just don't have time to see every actor who might decide to stop by.

In your cover letter, very briefly describe your training and experience, and mention that you'll call in about ten days to ask about coming in for an interview. Ten days leaves enough time between sending the letter and calling the office for the letter to arrive and get read.

When you call the office, be polite and not pushy. Ask if you might arrange a time to audition or to come in for an interview. If they tell you they're not seeing anyone at this time, ask when you might try again. Should you keep in touch with postcards? Be brief and businesslike—

remember that they're very busy. You don't want to be remembered as "that actor I can never get off the phone."

Don't let the people you contact scare you when they sound a little grouchy. But also avoid being so pushy that they never want to hear from you again. Try to walk the fine line between keeping them aware of who you are and making a pest of yourself.

AGENTS

The job of the agent is to schedule auditions for the actors who have made an agreement to pay them a portion of the money they make (a *commission*). These actors sign a written agreement, or *contract,* with the agent and are called the agent's *clients.*

The agent submits the photos of his or her clients to casting directors, producers, or directors for a chance at a particular role. Some agents give their clients advice on photos and also on things like clothes to wear, good grooming, and classes to take. Some are very good at giving support and encouragement to their clients. Some are not. And there are a few agents who tend to be abusive to actors, so it's a good idea to watch your step.

However, most agents are extremely choosy about the actors they will take on as their clients. Generally, they are interested in actors who already have a number of **credits** listed on their resumes that show that the actor has played noteworthy roles at quality theaters or in good films. Significant credits show the agent that the actor is already well on the way to a successful career. (See chapter R, "Resumes.")

Credits: The list on your resume of the roles you've played. Also refers to actors listed in a film—i.e., the opening credits, or the credits that run at the end of a film.

Some actors think that if they can get a good agent to represent them, they'll have it made and finally be able to relax. But an agent cannot get you a job. He or she can only arrange auditions and interviews for you. It will be up to you to get the job. And you'll have to get a number of jobs on your own before most agents will even be interested.

Again, let's say you're starting out as an actor. You contact agents the same way you contact casting directors: by mailing a photo and resume, waiting about ten days, and calling to ask if you can set up an audition or interview. It's best to notify agents when you have a good role in a show and send them a flyer two or three weeks ahead of time. One thing agents will do, when they have time, is come to see your work.

Like most people, agents and casting directors want to see good plays, as well as good acting work. They are not pleased if they come to a show that hasn't got much going for it. So you'll want to invite them only when you're sure the show is good—and only when you have a fairly large role and you're doing work that you're proud of.

A word of warning: actors always need to be careful about business matters. Some people in the industry realize how much young actors want to act and take that as an opportunity to "cash in." Be on your guard when any agent charges a set fee or asks for money up front. Agents are supposed to make money *only* when the actor is paid for his or her work. Their commission is usually 10 to 15 percent of the actor's total payment. Most of the time, there should be no other fees or charges—those with a good reputation in the business won't ask for money.

Some actors also seek representation with personal managers. A personal manager is generally much more involved in an actor's career than an agent, offering advice on image, promotion, and more. Their contract with the client often requires a higher commission, sometimes up to 25 percent, for the services they provide. Again, be very careful if you consider working with a personal manager, since they are not usually regulated by the unions as agents are. And a few can be pretty sleazy in their dealings with actors. Always ask around before you get involved with a personal manager, and be sure that you have someone who knows contracts, such as an attorney, read any contract before you sign.

WATCHING OUT FOR YOURSELF

Some agents will tell you that they charge a fee to put their clients' photos into books or on the Internet as a way to promote you to casting directors. Almost all of these kinds of excuses for charging you money are worthless. Many are invented to cheat actors. You can tell the agent you'd like to think about it, and if the agent pressures you right away to decide, you can be pretty sure something is not right. If an agent tries to sell you on the idea of a client photo book or website, ask to see a current copy. You can often tell by looking at the client photos whether it's something that would benefit you. And if the agent doesn't have something to show you, you'd be smart to pass up the offer.

Another good idea is to ask around to see if other actors you know have heard anything about a particular agent.

There are other "scams" that actors need to watch out for. Some actors have been approached by people saying that they know an easy and inexpensive way to get into one of the actors' unions. They'll collect a few hundred dollars from the actor (an amount that is way below the standard union initiation fees) and disappear without a trace. We all want to find easy ways to do things, but you should always think twice about a "bargain" like this, or a promise anyone might make to promote your career in return for money. If you smell something fishy, back away—you can probably trust your instincts. If you ask around, there's usually a way to find out if a situation is legitimate.

going to interviews
and auditions

Imagine you're a professional actor. You get home one day and discover that you have a message on your voicemail that Ms. Smythe, a theatrical agent, wants you to come in for a **general interview.** What do you do first? Run out and buy some new clothes? Brush up your favorite monologue? Let's look at what you would do as an actor with an important meeting ahead. You'll get a clear idea of what every actor goes through many times in the course of a career.

> **General interview:** An "interview" with someone in the business with the primary purpose of simply meeting, not usually for a particular role or project. An agent or casting director may call an actor in for a general interview if he or she is impressed with the actor's work or promotion package to meet the actor in person.

You call Ms. Smythe to set up a time for the interview. Try to be as flexible as you can—check your calendar before you get on the phone, and find several times when you could go. You should allow at least an hour for the interview, because other meetings before yours sometimes run late, so appointments may run behind. And you'd allow plenty of time for traveling to the office. Buses can often be late, and traffic slow.

A good actor knows how to be businesslike and brief on the phone. You want to tell whoever answers that the agent left a message for you. That way, the person on the other end knows you're someone the agent wants to speak to. Don't chat about the weather or the latest news, unless the agent does so first. Remember, agents are busy people, and you want them to spend time with you in person rather than on the phone. Make sure you have the time and date of the interview noted correctly in your calendar.

It's a good idea to have a few monologues prepared for an occasion like this. Be ready to do a variety: perhaps a comic monologue and one that's more straight drama. If you do classical theater, like Shakespeare, have a classical monologue ready. If you sing, have a few different songs ready. You never know what an agent might ask you to do!

TALKING ABOUT ACTING

Do you like to go to auditions?

Ric, age 16: *I hate it and love it all at once. I love the excitement and prepa-ration, and the feeling of elation that comes over me when I do something well during the audition. But I also hate it because I know someone is sitting there, analyzing and critiquing my every move, noting every mistake I make.*

If this feeling sounds familiar to you, try to focus more on the things you love about acting. Forget about feeling like you're being judged—that will only make you feel stressed out. It's hard to do well when you believe that someone is watching, comparing, and sizing you up. Think of an audition as a very short per-formance. If you have a way you usually help yourself feel at ease in front of an audience when you perform, use that same method in the audition, and let your-self "entertain your auditioner." Think of him or her happily sitting in a theater see-ing a show you're in. Also, trust in your training and experience, and try to have as much fun at auditions as you do onstage.

INTERVIEWING WITH AN AGENT

What do you wear to the interview? Clothes that look professional and feel comfortable. If you have a dress or a suit that people keep telling you looks great on you, wear that. Or wear your favorite piece of clothing, the one that always makes you feel special. You want to look good and feel just right, so you'll be at your best.

Do whatever you need to do before the interview to relax—do a vocal warm-up, or do some stretching exercises, or take a short nap or a walk— whatever works best for you.

Take ten or twenty copies of your photos along, with the resumes stapled on the back. If you have photo postcards, business cards, or a videotape of your work, take those along as well. And that calendar you bought to carry everywhere you go—don't forget that. It's unlikely you'll be setting up another appointment while you're in the office, but it won't look good if you need the calendar and don't have it.

Interviews can seem like such important events that actors get charged up or even scared. You want to carry a feeling of calmness and positive energy into the interview, instead of looking like you're in a hurry or overly excited. As you sit in the waiting room, take a few deep breaths. Tell yourself that, yes, the interview is important, but it's not the most important thing that will ever happen in your life. If it goes well, and the agent wants to work with you, great! It will probably open a new door in your career. If the agent doesn't seem as interested as you'd like, that's something you can live with. Everyone's taste is different—you may get along extremely well with one person and not at all with another. And there may be a good reason the agent isn't interested—perhaps he or she already has a number of clients that are similar to your type. You'll meet many more agents as you go along in your career, and one person's opinion is not all-important.

While you're there, notice what the office is like. Is it clean? Is there a cheerful feeling? You may not want to work with an agent if he or she has a messy office, or if there is a lot of tension in the air. Those qualities can interfere with an agent's ability to run a good business. And how does the agent make you feel? If you enjoy the meeting, you'd probably enjoy working with the agent. But if he or she makes you feel confused or unwelcome in some way, then it might be better to look for a different agent to work with. After all, you want to become a successful actor with a feeling that you're in control of matters like these—not to work with someone who makes you feel powerless or helpless.

Of course, you're friendly, and you answer the agent's questions honestly. You have a short answer prepared for what they always say: "So, tell me what you've been doing." Be prepared enough to know what you'd like to talk about. Think about the impression you'd like to make; don't just rattle off a list of your credits. Try sharing one of your favorite acting experiences or talking about a director you really enjoyed working with or the last role you played.

If you have questions, feel free to ask them. But don't keep thinking up more questions just to keep the interview going. When the agent seems to be wrapping it up, ask if you can keep in touch. Would it be okay to call once a week to see if any auditions have come up? Some agents like actors to call in and check. Others would rather wait and call the actor when they've set up an audition.

If the agent hasn't asked you to leave some photos and resumes, ask if you can leave some. Thank the agent, and as you leave, thank the receptionist or front-desk person, too. Why? People change positions often in agencies and casting offices. Next month that front-desk person could be working in a television casting office and might remember you.

Now, don't be surprised if you don't hear from the agent right away. A lot of agents like to have a wide range of actors to work with. They don't send you in for an audition until something comes up that they think you are truly right for. Sometimes an actor will interview with an agent but not hear from the agent for months. But then when the agent finally does call, the actor is perfect for the part that comes up.

Actors can't really expect anything to come of the interview. If something does, and you begin to work with the agent, it will be a bonus. This is one way actors deal with all the times they're turned down in their careers. If you build up your hopes with each interview or audition, every rejection will be a painful experience. But if you expect very little, you won't feel hurt if very little happens.

A meeting with an agent is usually an interview, as we've seen. A meeting with a casting director is mainly an audition. Let's turn to that now.

TALKING ABOUT ACTING

How do you feel about auditions?

Glenn, age 17: *When I audition for someone I know, I'm more relaxed, and I don't feel so pressured. It's easier because they already know what you can do. It's harder with someone I don't know, because I feel like I have to get my foot in the door.*

This is true for most actors. If you have auditioned in community theater or in school, you probably auditioned for people you know. But if you become a professional, particularly in a large city, you'll be auditioning mostly for strangers. You'll need to learn to be as relaxed as you can at auditions. Try some deep breathing, stretching, or imagining a quiet country setting, until you find a technique that works for you.

AUDITIONING FOR A CASTING DIRECTOR

There are several different types of casting directors. Some are on the staff of advertising agencies. They generally cast commercials. Some work for television networks and film production companies. And some work on their own on a project-by-project basis. Finding out as much as you can about the person you'll be meeting is a good plan.

You also want to learn what you can about the project you're auditioning for. If it's a new play, a commercial, or a film, find out if you can get the script a day or two ahead of time so that you can prepare. If it's a TV program, watch several episodes beforehand to get an idea of the style of the show and the different types of characters on it. If it's a published play, get a copy of it at the library or a bookstore and read it several times if you can. You can also check out the Breakdown Services, which provide **sides** for professional auditions, at www.actorsaccess.com (membership is currently free). The better prepared you are, and the more you know about the project, the more confident you'll feel. And you'll impress the casting person as a professional.

> **Sides:** The parts of the script you'll be auditioning with. Most often, they include the entire scene, but occasionally they will only include the actor's cue followed by the lines.

If you can, find out about other projects the casting person has worked on. If you've seen that film or play, you'll have a conversation starter.

At an audition, the smart actor would dress well and comfortably. Usually you'll have a few minutes to yourself after you arrive. Someone will likely be auditioning ahead of you, so you should try to find a private spot where you can warm up a bit and think. If you are auditioning with a monologue or a song, this is when you prepare so that you can slip quickly into character when your turn comes. (But bear in mind that you want to be yourself when you meet the casting director!)

If the casting director has you in mind for a particular role, he or she may give you some material to do as a **cold reading.** You could jump right into it, but it's probably best to ask if you can have a few minutes to look over the material. Then spend that few minutes making some

> **Cold reading:** Reading aloud a scene from the script without rehearsing, to see how you would fit with a role.

choices about the scene. In this case, your choices should be based on simple ideas. This is not the time to create a whole character you've never explored before, physically and vocally different from anything you've done. Ask yourself some simple questions:

- What does the character want?
- How is he or she trying to achieve this goal?
- What is the character really thinking while saying those lines?

Then relax and trust that your talent will come through when you perform the scene.

If you get nervous, remind yourself that an audition is simply a performance: it's a two- or five-minute scene that you perform for a tiny audience. It isn't the only chance you'll ever get; you'll probably go to hundreds of auditions during the course of your career.

One thing to remember is that the casting director is most likely on your side. Casting directors always appreciate well-trained, talented actors, and they hope you'll do a good audition and spark their interest. They like to discover new talent. If the casting director can present a number of interesting actors to the producer or director, it's a job well done. So don't worry about being judged. Just do your best and have a good time!

TALKING ABOUT ACTING

How do you feel about auditions?

Joe, age 17: *I love them! They're an exciting and suspenseful way of showcasing my talent.*

What a wonderful attitude! This young actor has found a way to take an experience that can be very difficult for some actors and turn it into something that excites and challenges him. This is an excellent example of real positive thinking—finding a new perspective on something that's difficult to make it work for you.

THE FOLLOWUP

After the interview or audition, send a thank-you note. If you can, pick out a detail to mention about the audition—something you really enjoyed, for example. Then begin sending the agent or the casting director your photo postcards. Every three to five weeks or so is enough to keep in touch. Let people know what you're doing. A lot of casting directors and agents will tell actors, "Keep in touch, even if you don't hear from me." That means they do have an interest in you and your work, but they don't have any roles in mind that you're right for at the moment. You never know when that role will come up that you're perfect for. If you've kept in touch, the agent or casting director will remember you and call you in to audition for it.

Sometimes the casting director is the one who follows up. When he or she thinks that an actor seems right for the role, that actor is given a callback to audition again. If that's the case, you want to wear the same or similar clothing to the callback as you did to the audition. Casting people sometimes find it easier to remember actors by the clothing they wear. In the callback audition, it's best to expand on the work you did at the first audition, rather than change your work altogether. After all, you were called back because they liked the work you did the first time!

how to prepare for a role

Whether an actor has been cast in a play or a film or is simply working on a monologue to use for auditions, he or she must know *how* to work on a role. This is why you need to learn some **characterization** basics. A good training program will help you learn the skills and techniques you need to pursue a professional career. You can get training through a college, university, or acting *conservatory* (school), or with a reputable teacher who has his or her own acting *studio* (workshop).

> **Characterization:** Preparing to act a role by deciding how a character looks, behaves, sounds, thinks, feels—and so on. Characterization is a very complex process that is generally taught in acting training programs.

Most professional actors continue to study over the years with a teacher or coach, always honing and perfecting their talent and craft. Even if you're planning on working in community theater instead of pursuing a career, taking an acting class can enhance your enjoyment of the experience of acting. It's a good place to try new ideas and make mistakes that you don't want to make in an actual performance. You can also learn quite a lot by watching other actors as they work.

Part of the magic of acting is making it look easy, and this takes a lot of skill, practice, and experience. Of course, good acting is *not* easy, so if you're thinking about moving to a major city to pursue a career, you owe it to yourself to get solid training (see chapter L, "Learning Your Craft").

GET TO KNOW THE SCRIPT

As a professional actor, the first thing you need to do, whether you've been cast in a role or you're working on an audition piece, is to become familiar with the script. You'll be creating a character and learning your lines later on; for starters, you need to understand the entire story, not just your own character's part in it.

Read the script several times and get a feeling for the theme—that is, what the author is trying to say. There was a reason the writer wanted to write the play, film, or TV show. Find out what that is. Ask yourself:

◆ Is the playwright trying to get a message across about the people in the play? About the situation? About the way the world is?
◆ What are the relationships between the characters like?
◆ Do any of the characters change, or see things differently, by the end of the piece?
◆ Are the characters "upper class," down-to-earth, or somewhere in between?

Try to get a feeling for the style of the script as well. Think about questions like these:

◆ Is it funny or sad or somewhere in between?
◆ Is it simple, or is there a lot going on throughout?
◆ Is there a lot of suspense? Does the story build and become more forceful?
◆ Is the dialogue elegant or slangy?

The more information you can get about the story before you start on your own characterization, the easier it will be to create your character, and the better your character will fit in with the whole piece. There are a number of excellent books on characterization that will add to your knowledge of this important skill (see chapter Z, "Zeroing in on Books," or check out the Drama Bookshop at www.dramabookshop.com).

What part of acting is most difficult for you?

Brian, age 16: *Breaking barriers of habit and never producing the same character.*

This is one of the aspects of acting that training and experience will help with. Training will broaden your understanding of acting styles and techniques and give you tools to create each character anew. And as you create and perform many different characters over time, you'll expand your knowledge of all the different aspects of characterization.

STARTING ON YOUR ROLE

One of the most important approaches to doing a role is to find a way you can "connect" to the character. You need to find some part of you that is touched by *who* the character is, or what the character wants or believes. You need to be able to understand why a character does what he or she does. Does this person do good works that benefit others? Or commit crimes to get what he or she wants? You would base your answers to these questions on your reading of the script.

One of the things actors love about their jobs is the unusual experience of "getting inside other people's heads." They discover sides of themselves they never knew existed and then use them to create a unique character. Through acting, you can portray a murderer or a saint, a president or a pauper—without any of the realities you'd have to deal with if you were actually that person!

To begin getting in touch with the character, ask yourself questions. As you gain more experience with characterization, you'll know quickly what kinds of questions will be most helpful to you. Here are some that most actors would start with:

◆ What's the most important thing that the character does in the play?
◆ Why does the character do what he does?
◆ What does she want most, and what lengths will she go to to get it?
◆ What are the character's relationships like? Close to other people or distant from them?

◆ Does he have any strong beliefs about himself? About the world? About other people?

◆ Does she get what she wants by the end of the play? What is her feeling about that?

◆ How do your character's actions and behavior connect with the author's theme or message?

You can think about some of the personal qualities your character might have:

◆ Do you think the character is impulsive, or deliberate and practical?

◆ Is he or she clever, or confused by the situation?

◆ Would the character be quick to help someone else, or more likely to manipulate others to get what he or she wants?

There are endless questions that you can ask to get a clearer picture of who your character is. These are just a way to begin, a way to stimulate your imagination.

The more thinking you can do about your character and his or her behavior and **motivation**, the more interesting your portrayal will be.

> **Motivation:** The reason the character performs the actions he or she does in the script. (Also see "Blocking," page 63.)

THE PHYSICAL CHARACTER

As actors gain experience, they learn different ways of expressing characters physically. Some characters move quickly, with a bouncy rhythm or nervous energy. Others move more slowly—some with care, some because they are afraid. If you sit in a mall for any length of time to watch people go by, you'll begin to notice that some walk swiftly, others with weariness. Some move smoothly and some jerkily. We learn to read others' body language very early in our lives, even if we're not conscious of what we're seeing. Sometimes you can almost guess what's going on in people's lives by how they move.

Along with rhythm, you can study posture: Does your character stand tall and move gracefully? Or does he or she stoop, or lean to one side? There are many possibilities for choices you can make about how your character moves and gestures:

◆ Is the character proud of who he is and what he does? (If he is, he would probably stand up straight and move with energy.)

◆ Or does he try to be noticed as little as possible? (This kind of behavior might result from fear. Or it might be a dishonest person's way of hiding something he did behind someone's back. Such a character might even sneak around.)

◆ Is the character generally in a hurry, trying to get too much done in too little time? Or is she relaxed, taking things as they come?

◆ Where would the character's worries show up in his or her body?

An actor must be careful not to make the physical choices too big or too obvious, or the character can end up looking more like a cartoon than a person. Some of the best physical work done by great **character actors** is so carefully performed that you hardly notice the details, which are often called *nuances*. They are subtle, but they still have an effect.

As you sharpen your own skill at observing people, you'll develop a sort of mental CD-ROM you can refer to for character "data." You'll also want to learn to listen to people's voices. An unusual voice can be the perfect finishing touch for a character. Here are some questions that can help you form an image of how the character behaves vocally:

> A **character actor** is known for creating unusual and interesting characters rather than acting in straight or leading roles. What great character actors in today's films spring to mind for you?

◆ Does he speak as quickly as possible? Is he afraid others will interrupt?

◆ Or does the character form thoughts and words slowly, speaking in a deliberate way?

◆ What area of the country is the character from? For instance, people from the South speak differently from other areas of the country. Characters have regional accents and dialects. And you can hear differences in the speed and pitch (highness or lowness of voice) with which they speak.

◆ Are the character's lips tight, as if she doesn't want to let the words out?

◆ Does she generally speak softly or loudly? (If softly, make sure the audience can still hear you!)

Again, don't make your vocal choices too obvious, so the character doesn't sound phony.

THE CHARACTER'S THINKING

As you can see, there are many details involved in building a character. An actor also needs to explore different ideas about how a character thinks:

- Does he have a quick mind?
- Does he make decisions only after much thought, or suddenly and impulsively?
- Is the character very intelligent, just average, or below average?
- Can the character see things through "other people's eyes," or only from her point of view?
- Does the character think clearly and correctly about the story's events? Is she confused, mistaken, or completely fooled?

There are many, many choices you can make about a character. As you make them, you *build* the character.

Some of the character's qualities will be fairly obvious after you've read the script a few times. Other qualities may take more digging. The director will point some out when you are rehearsing. You'll discover new choices when you are working with the rest of the cast. And there will be even more ideas you come up with to fill in the details that aren't suggested in the script.

The point is to explore. As a skilled professional actor, you'd explore as many possibilities as you could. Be sure that the choices you make for your character fit the script and the director's conception of the piece. As an actor, you want your performance to stand out, but not because it doesn't fit in with the rest of the play.

Near the end of the rehearsal period, you'll pretty much want to decide which of your ideas you want to keep and which to let go of. Once you're working in front of an audience or a camera, you'll be more comfortable if you have a fairly set structure that you've given yourself, and if you have a good general idea of what the other actors working with you will be doing.

in rehearsal

The process of rehearsing can be one of the most creative experiences you'll ever have. In the theater, you'll usually rehearse a play or musical for four to six weeks. The exception is in summer stock, where you may rehearse for only a week or two. In film, the rehearsal plan is usually set up by the director and may last from a few days up to several weeks.

LEARNING LINES

Different actors approach rehearsing in different ways. Some actors like to learn all their lines, if they can, before rehearsals begin. Other actors prefer to learn the lines during rehearsals as they learn the **blocking.**

> **Blocking:** Movement patterns given to the actors by the director to set up a specific "picture" that helps the audience understand the scene.

There are advantages and disadvantages to both methods. If you learn the lines first, you've completed a very important part of the process. You're free to use your rehearsal time in creating your character. But if you're not careful, as you learn the lines you may become too set in the speech rhythms and tones you've chosen. Then it can become hard to allow yourself to change as your character develops.

If you wait to learn the lines during rehearsals, you'll be learning your lines and blocking together and creating your character and working off the other actors, all at the same time. This can make it easier to put together many of the elements of your performance. If you choose this method, it's still a good idea to become as familiar with the script as you can before rehearsals begin. That way, you have a basic understanding of the story and the characters.

As you act more roles, you'll begin to learn how you work best. Each actor works in a different way, and once you find a way that works well for you, go with it. The work of performing and going to auditions and interviews can jangle anyone's nerves a bit, so actors are better off if they can find a reliable way of learning lines and creating a character.

BLOCKING

The blocking the director gives you can include crossing to another part of the stage or film set, entering or exiting the scene, and sitting down or standing up. The director may give you instructions such as "cross downstage right," or "sit in the up center chair."

Here is a diagram of the standard stage directions used in blocking:

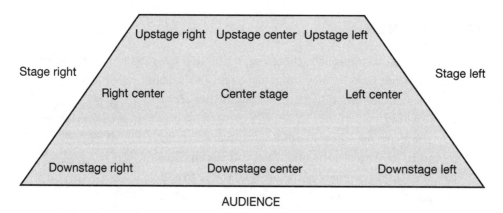

You'll notice that the directions of left and right are reversed from the viewpoint of the audience. When you're standing onstage facing the audience, "stage right" will refer to your right, "stage left" to your left.

The blocking in this scene is fairly unusual, but each actor has found a motivation to make his or her position make sense.

One important part of an actor's job is to find a *motivation,* or a purpose, for each piece of blocking the director assigns. That is, there must be a reason for the character to make that particular move.

For instance, if the director has given you blocking to stand up when another character enters the scene, you need to choose a good reason for your character to stand up at that time. Otherwise, you'll just look like you're standing up because the director told you to. Perhaps your character loves or hates the other character and is excited or dismayed to see that person. Or perhaps your character thinks of himself as a gentleman and rises whenever a woman enters. Or perhaps your character sees it's raining when the door opens and suddenly remembers she left the top down on her convertible, but she hasn't gotten what she wants yet in the scene, so she's torn between staying and going. The choice you make will dictate *how* you make the movement of standing up.

Choosing motivations is one of the most creative and fun aspects of the actor's work. Try different choices in rehearsal, to find out what works best for the character and the scene, you can experiment with simple and obvious motivations, and you can play with very complex or unusual ones. You'll usually know when you've found something that works. Something just "clicks"—with a good motivation, it "seems right" that the character stands or moves at that particular point in the story, and the blocking suddenly seems to help the action of the play, and the character's **objective**, move forward.

THE ACTOR'S CREATIVITY

The lines you speak and the director's blocking form the "skeleton" of the play, film, or show you're in. They're the elements that generally remain the same through the rehearsals and the performances. In the theater, you must always say the lines exactly as written, unless the playwright is present and chooses to rewrite them. The playwright has chosen those exact words for a particular reason. And unless the director is very flexible, you should perform the blocking without making changes.

> **Objective:** What the character most wants in a scene, or in the play or film—the goal of the character's actions. An actor usually comes up with a character objective for each scene and a larger objective for the entire play. Some examples are trying to convince another character that your point of view is the right one, persuading another character to do something for yours, or asking for help with a problem. You should work toward your objective as the character with all the energy you can muster, with "every fiber of your being."

What you can play with creatively as an actor are your use of your voice, your rhythms (faster or slower, with or without pauses), motivation, gestures, posture, and body language—anything that is not a part of the skeleton. Most actors like to play with choices quite a bit in the early rehearsals. They try a lot of different ways of doing things and then begin to firm up their choices as the rehearsals get close to the performance of the piece for the audience or the camera.

When a play is in performance, it runs much more smoothly if each actor knows pretty well what the other actors are going to do. Mistakes and odd moments will happen, but the more the rhythm of the show is set, the easier it is for actors to deal with things they weren't expecting.

On a film set, there is usually less rehearsal time available to play with different possibilities—so your own preparation work is that much more important. Work with different possibilities on your own so that you have several ideas in mind before the process of filming begins.

FEEDBACK FROM THE DIRECTOR

Directors will jot down notes during rehearsals and then read them back to the actors afterward. This is called *giving notes* to the actors. Basically, notes are the changes the director wants the actors to work on for the next rehearsal. These might include blocking changes, new ideas to try, lines that were spoken incorrectly, and character suggestions.

When the director gives you a note, you can ask questions if you need him or her to make something clearer. Then think about the notes and begin working on them as a sort of homework. The best actors always try to bring the change into their work in their next rehearsal.

Sometimes actors do not agree with the director. During notes is not the time to dispute with him or her. If you have a problem with one of the notes you're given, you must find a time to discuss it with the director in private. Just say "Okay," or "Thank you," and remind yourself to speak with the director later.

TALKING ABOUT ACTING

Is there anything you don't like about acting?

Iona, age 12: *I hate having an image of how I want to play a scene in my head, and the director is dead set on doing it a different way that I don't think works as well.*

This can be a problem at times. Sometimes the director is trying to achieve a vision of the play or film that you can't see from your view as a sole actor in the performance. It's hard to look at your own work from the outside. What you feel is coming across may not be what others see. Part of the director's job is to be another set of eyes, and the actor's job is to make good use of the feedback from the director.

Sometimes a director has a fixed idea of how a scene should go and won't give that up even if there is a better way. If you were in this situation, you'd need to find a time that you could talk with the director alone. The actor should never appear to be "showing up" the director, or making him or her feel put down in front of the whole cast. Ask if you can try the scene your way. Most directors will let you at least try, and some may see what you're trying to do.

As a very last resort, you might ask some of the other actors, privately, if they agree. They'll tell you whether you're the only one who feels as you do. But remember that the director does have the authority to make the final choices about scenes. You can explore to some degree, but if you change what the director told you to do on opening night or during filming, he or she probably won't want to work with you again.

The director's job is to bring about the best possible performance of the script. Sometimes the reason you get a particular note may not become clear for a while. It takes the cast some time to blend together into the finished performance, and the director has a view of the entire piece that no one actor can have. Sometimes you just have to trust that the director is doing a good job.

REHEARSAL ROUGH SPOTS

Not all directors are equally good. Sometimes major problems develop in rehearsals, and actors have to talk to someone whose advice they trust—a close friend, their agent, or a union official.

Directors are usually seen as powerful people, and sometimes they are. But they are not supposed to scream at actors, mistreat them, or put them down. If this happened to you in the rehearsal of a play, you could get advice on how to deal with it from the actors' union, Actors' Equity Association. In most union productions, the cast elects one actor who will represent them and act as a link to the union. You could take your problem to this person. You could have talks with people at the union office if the problem became very serious. If you had this problem on a film set, you could call the Screen Actors Guild (SAG) to ask for advice.

In rare cases, the union cannot solve a problem. Then, if you decided you could no longer work with the director, you could quit the show.

Problems are rarely so bad there is no way to work things out. But even among professionals, in the theater, in film, and in TV, things do not always go smoothly. Actors have unions they can turn to, and other people, too, when they need some help. You can read more about unions in chapter U, "Unions for Actors."

If you have a role in a nonunion production and run into a problem, talk to an acting teacher or someone else you trust for advice.

TALKING ABOUT ACTING

Is there anything you don't like about acting?

Howard, age 15: *The only thing I don't like about being in some shows is that some people in the cast don't seem to want to be involved in it. It's very frustrating—no matter what kind of part you have—to show up at a rehearsal for a play that opens in a week, and half the cast don't know their lines very well, and the other half don't even bother showing up.*

Good point! It sounds like the actors who don't show up don't really want to be actors. Or they don't have much respect for the director and the others in the cast. If you don't show up, you're wasting other people's time. If you were in a professional show, your behavior would probably get you fired.

TECH REHEARSALS AND DRESS REHEARSALS

In the theater, technical rehearsals—*tech* rehearsals, for short—take place in the last few days before opening night. Their purpose is to combine for the first time the technical elements of the production, such as the lighting, sound, scenery, and costumes, with the play. Everything can be examined for how it contributes to the whole. Equipment can be tested. Mistakes can be seen clearly, and the solutions to them can be discussed.

In early tech rehearsals, actors may be asked to stand in certain positions onstage while technicians adjust the lights. Another rehearsal may be spent getting used to the costumes and props. If you are rehearsing a script set in an earlier period in history, wearing clothing that will be similar to your costume in rehearsals can help you get a better feel for your character (e.g., a long, full skirt for women, a scabbard and sword for men).

In tech rehearsals, the primary objective is to pull all the elements of

If you are cast in a "period" play, it will be helpful to rehearse in clothing that is similar to what your costume will be like (a long dress, a judge's robe, and so on).

the show together into a whole and make sure that all of the technical aspects will work as they are meant to work. You may be running lines more than actually acting, and what you'll need most is *patience*. Often, actors may stand around in costume for long periods as lights and sound cues are adjusted and readjusted. But there's excitement in the air as well, because a new show is being born. This can be a good opportunity for you to run lines with the other actors if there are any scenes you're still unsure of.

If all goes well, the *dress rehearsal* will occur a night or two before opening night, and everyone will get a chance to feel what the real performance will be like. Much of the time, the dress rehearsal will feel bumpy and uncoordinated compared to other rehearsals, but this is a natural part of the process—it gets the kinks out before opening night.

Keep in mind as you work with the tech people that their contribution to the show is very important. Without costumes or light or props, the play would not be complete. The work that they do helps you do your best work as an actor.

In film and TV, the tech people are the camera operators, the makeup artists, the sound technicians, and so on. Actors owe these skilled people as much respect and courtesy as they would give the director and other actors.

The process of making a film or television program can be very much like an extended tech rehearsal: there you are, made up and in costume, warmed up, and standing around for forty-five minutes or an hour while the lights and camera are adjusted. The difference is that when the director says, "Action!" you need to be entirely focused and ready to do your best work.

Tech week and filmmaking can both be very strenuous and nerve racking. Actors working in theater need to take especially good care of their health as opening night gets closer. Everyone is excited during tech week. As the play goes through the last few rehearsals, everyone is gearing up for the magical time when the play comes alive in front of an audience for the first time.

the joy of performing

Imagine making your living as an actor. You might be working in film and television at times and on the stage at other times. The film and television jobs would pay you rather well, and you'd make good money if you booked a commercial now and then. When you're performing in film, you need to be able to "pop into the scene" the same way you do when you audition with a monologue. There's no live audience to feed your energy, but performing a scene on film using your talent and skill to create subtle nuances of behavior and feeling, and working with other actors who have the same attention to detail, can be very rewarding. With each subsequent take, you can slightly modify your work so that it becomes more truthful, more fascinating, and if all goes well, you'll end up with a wonderful performance that tells a captivating story about your character.

Working in the theater pays less well than film and television work, but it offers something special: performing in front of a live audience. This is what most actors live for—it's what makes all the hard work worthwhile.

In the theater, by the time the play opens you've worked hard for several weeks—learning your lines and blocking, working with props and costumes, and finally rehearsing under the lights. It's time to go out on the stage where many great actors have appeared before you and show what you can do!

BEFORE THE SHOW

Everyone is usually a little nervous on opening night. Dealing with costumes and props and remembering cues still takes concentration at this point. No one can predict how the audience will respond. This is a time when you must trust yourself as an actor. You have to feel that you've learned your lines and worked hard enough to know that the play will go well.

If there are things you're unsure of in the few days before the play opens, it's best to let the director know or spend a little extra time running your lines or scenes. Sometimes actors do need some extra rehearsal time to work out a complicated scene. You don't want to simply hope that, somehow, it'll come out right. The same goes with working in film: you want to be very confident about every aspect of the work so that you can truly give yourself to the moment while you're filming. If you've ever seen a show in which you can "see the actor underneath the role," you'll realize

With the help of the large mirrors in their backstage dressing room, these actors are putting on makeup before a performance.

that you very rarely ever see the *actor* in a film. You are watching the *characters* instead. It requires great confidence and great skill to act in films.

The director or stage manager gives you a call time to get to the theater for this opening night performance, and every other performance as well. Some actors like to get to the theater before the call time so that they have enough time to prepare. Unless there's a group warm-up, you need to make time while you're getting ready to warm up your voice and body. Sometimes actors like to do a warm-up when they arrive and then get into character while putting on their makeup and costume. Others put their makeup and costume on first and then warm up as close as possible to **curtain time.** As you gain experience, you'll find out what works best for you.

The stage manager gives you "warnings" before curtain time. These usually come a half hour, fifteen minutes, and five minutes before the show begins. That way you can pace yourself in getting ready. Next, the stage manager will ask for *places* at two minutes before curtain time. This simply means that he or she requests that you go to the place backstage from which you'll be entering. If you don't enter until later in the show, you may be able to wait in the dressing room or **green room** until a few moments before you enter.

> **Curtain time:** The time the show begins. This term is used whether there's a curtain in the theater or not.
>
> **Green room:** The traditional name for the room where actors wait before and between their time onstage. According to Wikipedia, the most widely accepted origin of the term dates back to Shakespearean times, when actors prepared for their performances in a room filled with plants and shrubs because it was believed that the moisture in the topiary was beneficial to the actors' voices.

OPENING NIGHT ENERGY

Now comes the moment you've been working so much for. You take a deep breath, relax, and let your energy and enjoyment flow. The more you enjoy being onstage, the more the audience will enjoy your performance. (If the play is a tragedy, you may not enjoy it in the same way, but you'll get caught up in the action.)

Opening night nerves are very natural. Forgetting a line or missing a moment may be a mistake, but it's not a disgrace. It's simply part of the process of putting on a play. One of the major reasons that audiences go to plays is to be entertained by live actors onstage, where anything can happen. So even though you may be very focused and working hard, mistakes sometimes occur. The best thing to do if someone makes a mistake is just to forget about it and go on with the play. The audience is there to see your live performance, not a perfectly timed, perfectly edited, perfectly set film performance.

You may have long stretches of time between scenes in which you appear onstage. You have to remember to keep your focus on the play even if you do other activities. Some actors read or play cards between their scenes. There are stories of actors who got so caught up in a card game that they missed an entrance. The actors onstage waiting for them had to **ad lib.**

Some actors ad lib very well; others have a more difficult time. The more familiar you are with your lines and character and the flow of the play, the easier it will be to ad lib when you need to. The main thing if you do have to ad lib is to carry on within the world of the play, so the action isn't taken to some new place from which you can't get back to the play.

Ad lib: Making up a line or lines on the spot. When an actor forgets a line, or is supposed to make an entrance and doesn't, the other actors can lose their place or have no way to continue the action if they do not invent dialogue or action. This is called ad-libbing.

An ad lib can be anything from what the weather is like to gossip about the character who will be coming onstage. Talking about the character who's going to enter creates a good reason to stop the instant he or she appears and then continue with the action of the play.

There are actors who become known for being late often or for missing their entrances. This is not a good reputation to have. Your career could suffer, because you might find it difficult to get cast again. Do your job with a professional attitude.

And have a good time, too! After that first performance comes the party that everyone's been waiting for: the opening night party. Now that you're past the jitters of opening the show, it will be even more fun!

TALKING ABOUT ACTING

What part of acting is hardest for you?

Jeremy, age 17: *The hardest part is how much of yourself you really have to use. Before I'd tried acting, I assumed actors were just reciting lines. But having done it now, it's a lot different. When I come home from having done an*

emotional scene, I don't want to do homework, wash dishes, or make my bed.
I just want to sleep!

Acting can take a lot out of you. And that's on top of the auditioning, which also takes a lot of energy. And then you have to make a living doing other jobs until you're earning money as an actor. If you're trying to figure out whether a career is a good move for you, think about the fun of rehearsals and the joy of performing. It keeps a lot of actors going. Will it be enough for you?

THE RUN OF THE PLAY

As you "run" the play over a period of nights, weeks, or months, you and the other actors will get more and more comfortable with the lines, the blocking, and each other. You'll probably find that you are deepening your character, just by being in the role night after night. Also, you will gain some freedom to play a little bit with things like your timing. You might:

◆ Make a move more quickly or slowly.
◆ Say a line faster or slower.
◆ Experiment with the length of a pause before an important line.

If you're in a comedy, even a millisecond change in the timing of a line can make a big difference between whether the audience just twitters or howls with laughter. (Of course, the action that leads up to the line is important, too.) Working with timing in comedies, and all kinds of plays, is one of the most enjoyable aspects of acting.

One change that actors are *not* permitted to make is to rewrite any of the lines in the play. And we've already seen that the blocking must stay the way the director wanted it. Making changes in these areas can start to throw the entire play out of whack.

Good actors always find that there's plenty of room to be creative with their character's behavior and thoughts. If you get a role in a show that runs for a year or more, you may end up fighting boredom more than the jitters. But remember: you can always go into more detail about what the character is thinking, what he or she believes, what he's trying to get, what she's really "all about." You should not let the show become a drag for you.

This is not a problem in acting in a film or TV show (unless you do a series that runs for many seasons). But in the theater, each person who bought a ticket should see the freshest performance you can give.

This is a good time, if you have a good role and the play is going well, to invite agents and casting directors. Sometimes, even when they're comfortable with the play and the performance, actors will get especially nervous if there are industry people in the audience. In this case, you'd want to do your best to forget that they're there—or remind yourself that they're just like the other members of the audience, sitting out there in the dark hoping to enjoy the show or see something meaningful. Just as you've learned to do in an audition, focus on how much you enjoy what you're doing, rather than on feeling "judged" for your performance or abilities.

keeping your balance

A cting is a business that has a lot to do with *personality,* so people in show business tend to put up with unusual personalities more than people in other fields, like banking and medicine, would. Because of this, show business sometimes attracts people who may be hard to work with or difficult to trust. Sometimes these people may hold positions of power—they may be directors or producers, casting directors or agents, or even teachers.

Let's say you're starting out as a young actor. It's helpful to know ahead of time that you may run into some difficult people or situations that upset you. This section is not intended to scare you away but to provide a reality check and show you why you need to be careful in dealing with people in your acting career. How do you keep your balance in this business?

TRUST YOUR FEELINGS

If you have a sense that something's fishy about a situation, your sense is probably correct. Your feelings can at least alert you that there might be a problem. Let's look at some possible harmful situations that could come up.

Suppose someone wants you to audition in a private home. Sounds odd, and unsafe, doesn't it? If you were in this situation, you'd definitely want to check around and make sure the person is legitimate before you go, or ask a friend to go along with you. Except in an emergency situation, most professionals wouldn't even consider holding auditions in their home.

Especially for women, if you live in a large city, it's best to be careful about where you go. In New York City or Los Angeles, there are some neighborhoods you'd want to stay away from. If you decide to move to a large city, ask a friend who's lived there a while which areas you should avoid.

Sometimes actors want to work so badly that they'll do almost anything. Then they run into difficulty. You don't want to be one of those actors who will risk their well being in order to succeed.

Any time people push you to do something you don't feel right about, such as auditioning at their residence or taking any of your clothes off, trust your instincts—one of the reasons you have them is to keep you safe. You don't ever have to do something that someone asks you to do if it doesn't feel right.

You may be asked to audition at night. Unless you know that the company often auditions at night—and there are some that do—you need to find out more about them ahead of time. The theater newspapers do their best to keep from printing any ads or casting notices that are not on the level, but sometimes one can slip through. Trust your instincts and ask other actors what they think.

WHEN THEY ASK FOR MONEY

There are people who cheat actors. Their tricks, or scams, aren't often dangerous, but you can lose money. Watch out for anyone who offers you a shortcut to getting something that normally takes some time when you follow the rules. One example is a union card. People have offered actors union membership cards, which actors usually earn by working in the business over a period of time. They say they know ways to get around the rules and then they take the actor's $600 or $1,000 and disappear.

You wouldn't want to believe any agent who says he or she will make you a star if you pay a certain amount of money up front. Some of these agents will tell you they'll put together a book of actors' photos that important producers will see, and this is what the money is for. Some honest agencies do create actor photo books, but anyone who promises to make you a star is only looking for your money.

Agents do business in connection with the actors' unions and have to follow the union rules. So the best way to find out if an agent has a good reputation is to call one of the unions. Actors' *managers* (also called personal managers) are different; they are *not* bound by any rules, so you'll need to be a little more alert when dealing with them. Ask for references from some of their current clients if you're unsure.

Actors just starting out often like the idea of hooking up with a theater company. These companies are usually small and may be called *acting troupes* or *ensembles* or some other name. But some companies will offer you membership only if you pay a certain amount of dues. This practice can be another fishy deal. There is no danger involved, but some professionals would tell you it's a mistake to pay people so that you can work for them.

Some of these small theater companies do fair work, but so do many of the companies where actors work for free. And many companies do pay actors something, even if it's just subway or bus fare.

If you are new to a city, becoming a member of a theater company can be a way to get to know other actors and get some experience. Just find out about a company before you join. If it has a bad reputation, stay away. Most of the casting directors and agents in the city will probably know that actors must pay to join and just won't bother to come see those performances. Go to see a couple of the company's performances—you can judge for yourself whether you think the work is good. To build a good reputation as an actor, you'll only want to work with companies that put on good shows.

Making a film or television show is often a very high-pressure situation. Directors need to bring the film in under deadline and on budget. For this reason, filming can often be much more stressful than working in the theater. But again, there is a line between the normal stress of the situation and feeling like someone is pressuring you or driving you unnecessarily. Over time, you'll learn what's normal on a film set versus when someone may be taking advantage of actors or mistreating them. Remember that the unions exist in part to ensure fair working conditions for actors. Don't hesitate to call them and ask if you're unsure about a particular situation.

Most people who work in the acting business are good people like you. You may never be in a harmful situation, but it's always best to be alert and be prepared if trouble turns up.

TALKING ABOUT ACTING

Do you have any advice for beginning actors?

Madigan, age 15: *Don't compromise yourself.*

This is a very good point. If you compromise yourself—which means if you do something that you don't believe in or that doesn't feel right to you—it can affect your self-esteem in a negative way. Don't let anyone talk you into anything that you know is wrong or anything that makes you very uncomfortable. If someone promises to get you an acting job or introduce you to people in return for a favor, think before you act. If it makes you feel funny, it's probably not on the level. Use your common sense, and keep good boundaries for yourself so that you don't get hurt.

HOW TO STAY SANE

Most of the people you meet as an actor will earn your trust. But some of them will make you wonder if you're losing your mind. As you know by now, show business does attract people who enjoy playing games with others. Some are on power trips and may mistreat you. Some directors, producers, and even acting teachers know that many actors will do almost anything to get a job. They feel powerful if they're in a position to offer the actor something, or to turn the actor down.

You can often spot these people long before they do you any harm. But some actors have a problem spotting them at first. Let's try to understand why this happens.

Some ways of being treated badly may be familiar to you. There is a lot of tension in some families. Parents may yell or say they're going to hurt someone. Even worse behavior can be considered normal in some families.

If this is true in your family, you may think it's acceptable behavior. It is not. And it is not acceptable in your work environment either. You don't ever have to allow anyone to hit you or threaten you. If anyone in your family, or anyone else, is yelling at you or calling you names, you have the right to walk away. This kind of behavior is abusive, and there are always better ways to settle things or to express anger.

Some actors have been screamed at in an acting class. Or they have worked with an agent or another person in the business who yells or threatens them. If this happens to you, remember: It is not because of any fault of your own. It's not because you've made a mistake. It's because that person enjoys putting other people down or is using actors to dump on as a way of expressing anger about something else.

The next thing you need to do is to get away from that person. And stay away. There are always more people to meet in the business—good, honest, caring people—and the more you move away from those who are bad news, the more you'll find people you'll really enjoy working with.

A teacher or an agent may threaten you with the idea that if you don't do what he or she wants, you'll never get another job as an actor. This is simply a game that person plays to feel like a big shot. If people like that can get you to believe what they're saying, then you're at their mercy and they feel stronger.

Usually, the reputation of someone like that is pretty well known to other people in the business. And that means the person has little or no real power with others.

It can be hard to spot a phony. If you were starting out and landed in a situation like this, it could be confusing to you. In that case, you'd need to find someone to talk to before you got stuck in a difficult situation. You could talk to a close friend who is also an actor. Or contact a teacher or college professor that you felt comfortable with. Talk about the behavior of the person who is confusing you or giving you a hard time. Ask for advice. Some people don't like talking about these kinds of issues and might brush you off. Keep trying until you find someone who will listen and help you.

TALKING ABOUT ACTING

What do you like about acting?

Lindsay, age 13: *The best thing about acting, for me, is being able to sort of "escape" so I can be someone besides myself for a change.*

This is something a lot of actors say they love about their work. They can try on different personalities as they explore new roles. Acting is a wonderful way to learn about yourself. Still, it's important not to think of acting as the only way you can express yourself. Some actors start to feel like they're not worth anything when they're not acting. You don't want to rely on acting to make you feel good about yourself.

You could also call one of the actors' unions, or a theater newspaper such as *Back Stage*. You would ask them to refer you to someone. You could call the Actors' Fund, another organization that helps actors—the people there will listen and can help you understand and cope effectively with just about any situation (see chapter W, "Working the Web," for more information on this and similar organizations).

Just don't let a situation go on until you feel like you can't get out of it without getting hurt. Actors sometimes feel that everyone else is in charge of what happens to them, or think they have to do whatever someone else says if they want to get work as an actor. But if you ever land in a situation where you are being mistreated, you must not be afraid to say, "I have to leave now." You can be in charge and walk out. People you don't want to work with can't hold you back from getting other jobs someplace else.

A career in acting can be very rewarding, but not if you have to work with negative people. Do your best to stay focused on the healthy and the positive, and take care of your well-being. You'll stay sane and have a better chance of success.

learning your craft

We've already said that an actor needs good training. Having well-developed skills and a technique that works for you is essential if you decide you want to be a professional actor. The truth is, many actors continue to work on their craft even after they've begun to make a living. Let's discuss the first training you can get as an actor and then look at the ways you can continue with your training.

TRAINING IN HIGH SCHOOL

If you're serious about having a career as an actor, you may be able to go to a performing arts or Magnet high school. It's to your advantage to begin your training as early as possible. Competition at performing arts high schools can be strong, and you'll need to keep up your grades just as you would at any other high school.

You can find out more about Magnet high schools that have performing arts programs by going to www.magnet.edu. Although the schools are not in state order, you can search through the listings and may be able to find a school near you. You can also search by typing "high school of performing arts" and a city near you in the search box.

Many regular high schools also have good theater classes or clubs.

Even if you're not in high school yet, check to see if your local high school has a drama club. This is a good way to get started acting and meet others who like theater.

High school theater classes can give you some good first lessons in acting. But you may also want to get some training that goes deeper. You can check the yellow pages to see if there are any after-school theater classes or programs for young people in your area.

Or you might do some work or act a role at a nearby theater. It might be a professional theater, but it will probably be a community theater. Many of the adults who do community theater have been acting and directing for years, and you can learn a lot by watching and acting with them. You'll want to see as many shows as you can, too. Sitting in the audience, you can learn what makes you believe an actor's performance. And you'll begin to figure out what doesn't work, as well.

If you're already in high school, ask one of your teachers about the Arts Recognition and Talent Search. This program is run by the National Foundation for Advancement in the Arts. They award scholarships to high school seniors in theater, musical theater, dance, music, the visual arts, and writing. The students who get the awards may get a chance to go to a major acting school, such as the Juilliard School or New York University, both in New York City. If you participate in this program, you have a better chance of getting your career off to a running start.

You can get more information about the program at their website, www.nfaa.org, or you can write to them at:

National Foundation for Advancement in the Arts
444 Brickell Avenue, P-14
Miami, FL 33131

TALKING ABOUT ACTING

Is there any advice you'd offer to young actors?

Linda (a young actor who has started her career), age 24: *Go to college! That way, if the whole showbiz thing doesn't work out, you have a degree of some sort to fall back on.*

If you're not able to attend a performing arts school, it's still a very good idea to go to college, wherever you can. Going to college to will give you a broader understanding of the world. The more you know about different subjects and ideas, the better your acting will be. Getting a college degree can also be very helpful in getting a job that supports you while you look for acting work.

And, of course, you want to start thinking ahead: should you study acting in college or in an acting program at a special school, such as a performing arts institute or conservatory? College or university training, or some kind of long-term, in-depth program, is extremely important if you're thinking of pursuing a professional career—it will give you a solid grounding in the art and an acting technique you can depend on.

TRAINING IN COLLEGE

Your best bet for college, if you're planning to be a professional actor, is to go to one of the schools that are part of the National League of Professional Training Programs. These schools have set up their programs to give the best training possible to actors who will be pursuing a professional career. Here is a list of some of them (you can also find their web addresses in chapter W, "Working the Web"):

American Conservatory Theatre, San Francisco
Boston University
Carnegie-Mellon University, Pittsburgh
The Juilliard School, New York City
New York University Tisch School of the Arts
North Carolina School of the Arts, Winston-Salem
Southern Methodist University, Dallas
State University of New York at Purchase
Temple University, Philadelphia
University of California–San Diego
University of Washington School of Drama, Seattle
Yale School of Drama, New Haven, Connecticut

These schools train actors to become professionals and then give them a chance to audition for agents and casting directors near the end of the

This director is working closely with actors in rehearsal. If you were to go to a school that is connected with a professional theater (see "Learning Your Craft," page 84), you'd probably get to work with professional directors.

program. If you can go to one of these schools, you'll have a much better chance of getting your career off the ground in the beginning. Most agents and casting directors have a high regard for graduates of these schools. This doesn't mean that if you go to a different college, you don't have a chance at building a good career. But these schools can get you started a little bit faster.

Some of these institutions offer MFA (Master of Fine Arts) programs as well as undergraduate degrees. If you are seriously considering a professional career, you will be a step ahead of many actors if you attend an MFA program after your undergraduate training—in terms of the experience you'll gain, the contacts you'll make, and the esteem that is given to MFA graduates by others in the acting business (i.e., you'll start out with professional credentials rather than having to build them piece by piece). Although it may seem like getting professional training is a step you could skip, it can really make a difference in the success you can achieve as a professional actor.

TALKING ABOUT ACTING

What part of acting is most difficult for you?

Joe, age 15: *Replicating raw emotion in the moment.*

This is another reason that training is so important. When you play a role night after night in the theater, or scene after scene in a movie, you need to know how to access your emotions, create a sense of place and relationship, and make the situation believable to yourself so that it's believable to your audience. This takes training (so you have some tools to make it happen on demand) and experience (practicing over time so that you're confident you can make it work whenever you need to).

Another plan is to go to a theater training program that is not part of a regular university. These kinds of programs are also geared to actors who will pursue a career. Some are members of the National Association of Schools of Theatre. These schools offer two- or three-year programs. Most are located in a large city, so you'll learn all about living in one before you even begin your career. You can search for an accredited theater school near you by going to their website (http://nast.arts-accredit.org/).

Here is a list of some of these schools—you can write to them or search for them online to find out what they require to get in:

American Conservatory Theatre
30 Grant Ave., 6th Floor
San Francisco, CA 94102

Neighborhood Playhouse School
   of Theatre
340 E. 54th Street
New York, NY 10022

New Actors Workshop
259 W. 30th Street
New York, NY 10001

Circle in the Square Theatre School
1633 Broadway
New York, NY 10019-6795

National Conservatory
   of Dramatic Arts
1556 Wisconsin Ave. NW
Washington, DC 20007

National Shakespeare Conservatory
440 Lafayette Street
New York, NY 10003

National Theatre Conservatory
1050 13th Street
Denver, CO 80204

Eugene O'Neill Theater Center
305 Great Neck Road
Waterford, CT 06385

Boston Conservatory
8 The Fenway
Boston, MA 02215

ANOTHER NETWORK OF SCHOOLS

There is another network of theater schools, the University/Resident Theatre Association. U/RTA-affiliated schools offer actors an exceptional opportunity to work with professional theater companies during their training. Although the U/RTA program is geared to current undergraduate university students who are planning to continue their training in a master's degree program, most of the affiliated schools do offer undergraduate degrees. One of the best things about them, aside from the opportunity to work with a professional company, is that you can audition for a large group of master's degree programs and resident theater companies all at one time. People from the schools and the companies gather once a year in New York, Los Angeles, and Chicago to see actors audition.

You can find out more about the University/Resident Theatre Association by visiting their website: www.urta.com.

You can also search on the web for "accredited theater schools" or "professional theater training programs." Get as much information as you can about any training program you're thinking about. Your early training will form the basis for the acting technique you use throughout your career.

As you search the web, you may notice a number of acting classes advertised that you can take over the Internet. Although you might gain some knowledge from these kinds of programs, they are no substitute for real-time, in-person acting classes. If you're serious about becoming an actor, you need to work with a teacher who can watch your acting work in person and guide you to better use of your skills and talent; and you need to be learning to work in-depth with other actors. You can't learn to act over the Internet.

SUMMER CAMPS FOR YOUNG ACTORS

Summer theater camps geared to young actors exist all over the country. This is another way to get a head start on training (and have fun!) before you begin university or theater school training. Two of the most well known are Stage Door Manor in Loch Sheldrake, New York (www.stagedoormanor.com) and Walden Theatre in Louisville, KY (www.waldentheatre.org).

Both of these camps hold several sessions each summer running from one to three weeks, culminating in a professional-quality production at the end of each session. Stage Door Manor invites theater professionals from New York City and L.A. to teach classes and workshops, so space is very limited, and you must sign up early. Walden Theatre also offers professional conservatory-style classes. You can download information about these camps from their websites.

Almost any summer camp will offer you the opportunity to learn and perform. Find out as much as you can about any camp you're thinking of attending, just as you would gather information about agents or theaters if you were a professional actor. Camp is a good opportunity not only to learn and have fun but to start building your network of fellow theater enthusiasts.

ACTING CLASSES

Whether you're taking classes to polish up your skills as an actor or taking classes just for fun, there are many kinds of teachers and classes to choose from. In most classes, you'll work on acting by doing scenes from plays, films, or commercial scripts.

Acting classes aren't all the same. There are classes in improvisation, acting technique, and scene study. There are also classes in different *period*

An actor needs to start training before beginning a career. Even if you have already had training, look into a class that meets one or two nights a week. As time goes by, it's a good idea to go on taking acting classes—and occasionally to try a class in a different area, such as movement or dance.

styles—that is, historical periods. For example, Shakespeare's plays are period plays, and to do them well you need to learn how people moved and behaved many centuries ago. And there are film and commercial technique classes that teach you special skills for performing before a camera.

Every teacher has his or her own style or method. When you're beginning to learn acting, it's a good idea to take classes with several teachers. This way you can get a feel for how different teachers approach acting. Then you can decide to study with one of them. Finding a teacher that you work with well is like finding a good friend: it takes some time to get to know that teacher. Usually, you'll feel more comfortable with some than with others. You'll be able to tell after a few weeks of classes whether the teacher is helping you to grow.

Most acting classes run for several weeks or several months. Teachers of technique will teach you some steps to take in developing a character. Often, you'll learn about your **sense memory** and how to strengthen it. In the first meetings of an acting class, the teacher will often take you through some exercises and then will begin to teach you acting technique. The teacher might suggest a specific monologue for you to work on and bring to class, or you might be asked to work on a scene with a partner outside class and then perform it in class so that the teacher (and sometimes the other students) can comment and make suggestions. Usually you and your partner will begin by performing the entire scene for the class. Then the teacher may work with you on specific sections of the scene, which are also called *beats*. Or he or she may help you work on your character or relationship in some other way.

Many good actors think of acting classes as a place to take risks, to play, to try different ways of doing things. It's better to try a new approach and have it work poorly in the class than on a job that you've been hired for. If you watch the work of the other actors in the class, you can learn a lot about

Sense memory: When you recall an experience you stored in your memory and use it in your acting, you are using your sense memory. For example, in some scenes you may need to act being cold. Your senses have been affected by cold in the past, so you begin reacting the same way, based on your memory of that moment—by shivering or rubbing your hands. In a more advanced use of sense memory, you might use a recalled feeling of how you respond when someone is yelling at you in a particular scene in which your character is extremely upset (even though there may not be an actual argument occurring in the scene). Actors' performances are more realistic when they use their past sensations as tools in this way.

what works in a scene and what does not. Pay attention to the other actors and you might notice someone you'd really like to work with because of his or her talent, skill, or style. You can ask the teacher to assign a scene for you to work on together.

As you get more training and experience as an actor, you'll find out which techniques work well for you and which do not. If an actor tried to use every acting technique, his or her performances would be nothing but a hodge-podge. So use what works for you and forget the rest. Actors need to develop their own style as they go along and learn to trust their inner sense of what is right.

Taking an acting or **scene study** class is a good way to learn the self-discipline a professional actor must have. If you're working on a scene with a partner outside class, take care not to goof around and neglect your work. Remember, the actors you see on the stage and screen do a lot of outside work on their roles. They are usually extremely disciplined. You'll get much more out of your acting classes if you work hard even when you're not there, learning the craft of acting on your own. And if you'll be going into acting as a career, the better your acting is, the better your chances of being hired will be.

If you are considering a professional career, it would also be a good idea to take a **business class** for actors. This kind of class will help you learn what casting directors and agents are looking for, how to promote yourself as an actor, and how to keep the business side of your career running smoothly.

Scene study: In this type of acting class, the teacher asks you to pick a scene from a play or assigns you a scene and helps you and a partner work on it. Then, any work you do on your acting technique is done when it's needed in that scene.

A **business class** can teach you how to organize your career as a business and help you set up a self-promotion plan so that you're clear on the tasks needed to get work as an actor.

money and work

Money can be a difficult subject for actors to think about. Maybe you've heard a lot about how hard it is for actors to make a living. It is true that most professional actors cannot get by on acting jobs alone. Most of them must find other jobs to make enough to live on, so that they can do what they love: acting. If you're thinking of pursuing a career, you need to take a realistic look at the subject of money. As an actor, you too will probably be doing other jobs to make money at the same time as you pursue your career

BELIEFS ABOUT MONEY

Let's start out with two beliefs that will help you think about the money side of your acting career. The first belief is, if you believe in your heart that you *can* make a living at acting, you will have the right attitude for success.

The second belief is, if you believe in your heart that you'll *never* make a living at acting, you never will. Why? Because that's how you'll make your efforts turn out, consciously or unconsciously.

It's not easy to see reality clearly and yet not fall into the trap of expecting to be poor just because you're an actor. It's important that you don't stick yourself with a *not* belief: that you're *not* going to have any money. *Not* beliefs of this kind that get set in your mind can be found in every area of your life, if you look for them:

◆ "I don't have any fun."
◆ "I can never find a nice boyfriend/girlfriend."
◆ "My hair always looks messy."

If there's something you don't like about your life, say to yourself, "That's a problem," and then look for ways to improve it. Don't just assume your hair is going to be messy for the rest of your life! There are many steps you can take to solve almost any problem.

When it comes to money and work, you need positive beliefs. The trick is to allow yourself to have as much money as you want and need, even though you're an actor. It can be done, if you look ahead.

MAKING A LIVING

We often hear about actors who hit it big and make enormous amounts of money. None of them could have started out being sure they'd get rich. It's smart to assume you will not make your living right away as an actor.

So, what other things do you like to do that might support you while you build your career? Remember that becoming an actor will take a certain amount of money for classes and photos. And it will take a lot of time to go to interviews and auditions and work on monologues and roles. So you'll want some kind of job that pays you well, offers a flexible schedule, and allows you some free time for auditions.

Many actors support themselves as waiters. If you get hired at a top-quality restaurant, the tips can be enough along with the salary to give you the money you need. Other actors work as secretaries, word processors, and proofreaders in jobs they got from a temporary agency.

"Temp" jobs can be an excellent way to support your acting career. Working with a **temporary agency** gives you a lot of flexibility. In large cities they may pay pretty well if you have good skills. And it's usually easy to get work with temp agencies, even if you've

Temporary agency: A "temp" business has a number of client companies and hires you for only a day, a week, or a month to work at one of those companies.

had to take some time off for acting work. Look in the yellow pages under "Employment Agencies—Temporary" to see if there are any in your area.

If you're thinking of moving to one of the major cities, make it a point soon after you move to visit the agencies and apply for work. You can register with several different agencies. This will bring you more chances to work when you want to, and you won't be tied down to one agency. If this idea is more appealing to you than waiting tables, find a way before you hit the big city to develop useful skills: typing, computer skills, and proofreading can virtually be learned on your own with some determination and practice.

A lot of actors like the variety they get from working at temp agencies. You may work at a bank one week, a law firm the next, and so on. If you prefer the idea of waiting tables, learning how waiters serve people at fine restaurants and getting some credible experience before you go will help you find work without a lot of trouble.

Some actors create their own businesses. They go to school and get licensed to give massages, or deliver singing telegrams, or take care of people's pets, and so on, as they pursue their careers. This can be a great approach, because if you have your own business, you can work when it fits into your day. The only thing to be careful of is spending all your time and energy building up that business. You can lose sight of what you wanted to do with your acting career. Of course, if the business begins to do very well, and you're enjoying yourself, giving up your acting career is a viable option.

As you can see, it helps to know how you'd like to support yourself before you begin a career.

THE NUMBERS

If you're a young person, you might not have much experience with money yet. Parents don't often share a lot of news about the bills they're paying. How much money will you need to pay the bills each month if you live in New York or Los Angeles? Here is a list of basic monthly expenses:

Rent $1,000 and up—way up!
                        (cheaper if you share with others)

Groceries	$100 and up (doesn't include eating out)
Gas and electric bills	$60 and up
Transportation	$100 and up
	(subways in New York; car in Los Angeles)
Telephone	$50 and up
Personal care	$40 or more, depending on your needs (soap, shampoo, toothpaste, etc.)

The total for one month is $1,375! And these are just the very basics you need in order to live—it leaves out costs for:

◆ Home furnishings
◆ Health insurance (if you're not covered by your job, which you probably won't be)
◆ Any medical or dental expenses that aren't covered by insurance
◆ Entertainment
◆ Eating out
◆ Taking care of a car (if you have one), car payments, etc.
◆ Promoting yourself as an actor
◆ Presenting yourself well: haircuts and clothes

In other cities—Chicago, Seattle, or Denver, for example—the costs will be lower than in New York or Los Angeles, but not much. And remember: taxes will take out around one-fourth of the money you make, usually before you even get your paycheck.

If you're pursuing an acting career, you'll be spending money on these things, too:

Photography session	$200 and up
Copies of your photo	$75 and up per 100 copies
Resume copying	$10 per 100 copies
Photo postcards	$75
Postage	$30 and more every month
Classes	$25 or more per class (acting, voice, movement); better classes are usually more expensive

Reading	$20 or more a month
	(books, newspapers, scripts)

As you can see, the need for money quickly adds up! And when you're ready to join one of the unions, the fee will be close to $1,000. After that you'll pay dues of $35 to $50 a year.

These numbers aren't meant to scare you or make you give up acting. You just need to know ahead of time how important it will be to have enough money to live comfortably while pursuing a career. It does not need to be difficult. For instance, if you're earning close to $100 a night from restaurant work, you'll have enough for your basic monthly needs in about seventeen working days (even enough to pay your taxes). After that, the money you earn can go toward your career. If you work four to five shifts a week, that adds up to sixteen to twenty working days per month.

You'll have to support yourself for months or years as you begin your acting career. And it's much easier to do some thinking about what kind of work you'd enjoy before you find yourself in a situation where you have to get work in a hurry. If you plan to be a professional actor, spend some time planning how you can support yourself apart from acting in a comfortable, enjoyable way.

TALKING ABOUT ACTING

Do you think you'll be a professional actor?

Megan, age 12: *I probably will do something with entertaining people, because I don't think I can picture myself doing anything but that. But I don't want to starve, either.*

Does this sound like she's starting to tell herself before she even begins that she will not have what she wants? When it comes to money, it's good to have your eyes open to reality. But if you believe that your only choices are: "I can do what I want and be poor," or "I can do something I don't like and not be poor"—then you're setting yourself up for a fall. The truth is, you can be an actor and have money. You just need to plan carefully how you will support yourself.

HAVE FUN WITH YOUR LIFE, TOO!

It's not easy to work on your career or do anything well if you're always worried about paying the rent or eating. You need to find a way to make enough money so that you can enjoy your life. You may need to give up some things you like so you can be an actor, but if you have to do this for many, many years, it's possible to get depressed. That can make pursuing your career even harder. Find a way to make enough money so that you're not feeling needy.

Your hopes for enjoyment should not be tied up in your acting career only. Find some time to do other things you enjoy—to be with friends and to develop your life in other ways. If you base all your hopes on your acting career, but don't reach the success you wanted, you may end up feeling bad about life or disappointed in yourself. It's extremely difficult to be a professional actor, so you need other activities in your life—and other people besides actors. Those other sources of joy will keep you feeling good and give you energy as you go.

The same can be said of any career you might choose: the more things you have in your life outside your work that you enjoy, the happier and more successful you're likely to be.

chapter **N**

networking

I t's often said in life that it's not what you know, but *who* you know that makes the difference between minor and major success. This is true in any business, but even more important in an acting career. Many people who are stars today are related to, or have close connections to, other actors, agents, directors, and producers.

This means that show business is not really fair. It's natural for people to feel more comfortable working with someone they know than trying out a new face. Some directors have taken a chance on a new actor only to wish they had chosen someone they were more sure of. Often, there might be two actors a director is considering for a role. He might like the possibilities offered by a newcomer. But if he liked working with one of them a lot, and has never met the other, he will probably cast the actor he has worked with. The world of show business is crazy enough as it is—people would generally rather work with actors they know they can depend on than take a chance with an unknown person.

Networking is the term used to describe people's system of getting to know each other for the sake of their careers. Part of networking is talking to other people in your career field and finding out what they do. If you can get another person to be aware of you, that person may tell others about you or tell you about people they have met. As a result, you make links to a number of other people in your profession—people you might never have met and who might be able to assist you. Over time, the links keep growing, and by keeping in touch with the people you've met, you create your own network.

Let's see how an actor networks with others in the business.

BE YOURSELF

Young actors starting out often try to be someone they are not, striving to make a good impression on others. Acting is a business based on performing and acting, so some actors think they have to play a character even when they're at a party or meeting others. But networking is really about making honest connections. You really want to know people on the basis of a shared love for the performing arts. If you're being phony, or trying to be someone other than who you are, most people will notice. They may not be interested in getting to know you further or working with you.

You probably have noticed a phony attitude in someone you know at school, or you might get a funny feeling when you're around a certain person. You can tell that person is straining to create a look, or is stretching the truth. Ever notice how difficult it can be to have a conversation with him or her? Well, professional show-business people will know if you're putting on an act, so it's best to be yourself. Just aim to be the best self you can be.

It can be hard sometimes to be yourself. We all have doubts and fears about who we are. Although you want to be confident in your skills and about yourself, it's not possible to feel strong and happy all the time. But one of the ways we connect with other people is through our ability to feel all kinds of emotions. When you're networking to pursue your career, it's easy to forget about the human side of the relationships. You don't want to see people only as a way to get what you want. Nobody wants to be treated as just another stepping stone to your success.

The performing arts are based on our feelings, hopes, and beliefs, so your relationships with other people in the business need to be based on your shared human qualities. You might be feeling nervous at an audition, but a casting person might also be feeling nervous that he or she won't be able to find actors who will please the director. You wouldn't mention it to them, but it might help you to relax a bit if you know they may be nervous, too.

Agents and casting people are human, just like everyone you've always known. So make your links with people from your heart and soul.

HOW TO NETWORK

The best way to begin learning how to network is right in your own area. You can start out with local theater activities. Read the arts section of the newspaper for a while to find out which theaters put on shows and what kinds of shows these are. Does one director's or actor's name keep popping up in the articles you read? That person might be a good person to meet and talk to. As a way to practice, the next time you see that person's name, try to go see the show he or she is connected with. If you liked the show, go backstage and tell that person.

This can take courage. But remember this: actors and other show-business people love to hear what you liked about their work. He or she will probably be delighted to hear your comments. This is not a time to be pushy or to ask if any jobs are coming up. This is simply your first meeting. The next time you see that person's name in the news, go see his or her latest show and begin to develop that first contact into a friendship if you can. Eventually the person will probably ask about what you're doing. If you're in a show, tell them about it. If you're not, say, "I'm between roles right now. My last show was...," and talk about that. Be brief and friendly. If you chatter on and on, they probably won't ask you again the next time.

If you read the theater publications, or **trades**, as often as you can, some names will become familiar. After a while, if you go to audition for a play that's being directed by Don Jonas, you'll know from reading the trades what Mr. Jonas has directed in the last year. If you saw any of his work, you can talk with him for a minute or two about the play or the production, and you've entered into the world that he knows. You've made a contact.

> **Trades:** The nickname given to theater publications such as *Hollywood Reporter*, *Variety*, and *BackStage*.

TALKING ABOUT ACTING

What do you think it would be like to be a professional actor?

Ned, age 15: *It would be tough looking for new work! You have to look through the paper every time you're not doing something. And going someplace new, like New York, where you're not known at all—it seems like it would be really tough. Everyone else is as good as you are, if not better. And they already have experience there.*

Yes, as a newcomer, you have to work twice as hard just to get noticed. When you move to a new place, it's best to build your career one step at a time. If you expect to be an overnight success, you'll probably get so disappointed it will be harder to do the work you need to do. So don't expect to get your first job right away. In the beginning, take classes and get to know people.

Another thing to remember is that it can take years for some of these first contacts to grow into a chance that you might work together. At times, an actor makes such a strong impression that a director or casting person will think of him or her for a certain role that's coming up. But you must be prepared to continue your networking for many months or years.

If you're going to an audition for a play or film, try to find out who the director is. Then look him or her up online and find out what he or she has done recently. See the film or read the play (perhaps there is also a review of the play you can read). You'll have an instant conversation starter: "Didn't you direct *The Merry-Go-Round* last year? I saw that, and I thought it was an excellent production." Of course you only want to mention plays or films that you actually have seen—how embarrassing it would be to have a director ask you about a particular scene or character and have no idea what he or she is talking about. Be honest in all of your dealings with people in the business, and you'll gain a good reputation.

Once you've made the first contact, ask if you can keep in touch with the person. You can send a photo and resume to start, then follow up with a photo postcard in a few weeks, or a flyer for a show that you're in. (You'll read more about sending out your promotional material in chapter Q, "Questions About Promoting Yourself.")

Whenever you get a new photo and do a new resume, send them. Send a greeting card or a holiday message! But bear in mind that many other actors contact directors and other people in the business as well. You'll probably need to keep in touch for a long time. If you can find a way to make your mailings stand out from the others—but without getting weird—try that.

You'll also need a method to keep track of the people you're contacting. Computers are very handy for this, especially the mail merge function. You can put the name of a new person into a database and then write letters and prepare your labels or envelopes. If you don't have a computer, you can keep the information on paper, with a list that includes:

◆ The name of the person you contacted
◆ The date you sent the person information
◆ What you sent (photo, flyer, etc.)
◆ Whether you received a response (see page 41 for a chart that you can use)

A NETWORKING ACTOR

Let's follow Mark, the actor from "A Day in the Life of a Professional Actor" (chapter D), as he networks his way into a role. Mark has decided to take an acting class with a teacher in New York that he's heard good things about. After several weeks, he finds out that one of the other actors in the class, Alan, is appearing in an off-Broadway show. He likes the work Alan does in the class, so he goes to see the show. Afterward, he goes backstage to tell Alan how much he enjoyed the performance.

The next week in class Mark asks Alan if he would do a scene with him for class. Alan says yes. They begin work on a scene, and a few days later Alan says he's auditioning for a new show. He invites Mark to come along.

At the audition, Alan introduces Mark to the director, who knows Alan. Mark does a good job of reading from the script. The director likes Mark's audition, but he doesn't have a role for him in this show. Still, he calls another director who does need an actor of Mark's type to fill a role—one that a cast member had to give up because of illness. The second director calls Mark in for a brief audition and casts Mark on the spot!

Mark has to work hard because the show opens in a week, but his training helps him get ready and act the role well.

This is an extreme example—in most cases, your networking won't pay off so quickly. Our friend Mark, if you'll remember, put quite a lot of time and energy into his career before this break came about, and of course he was well trained and ready for the challenge. But breaks like this do happen occasionally. And you can see from this example how each person you meet may introduce you to other people, who may tell others about you, and so on. That's networking.

So keep a list of people whose work you enjoy and respect, and try to keep up on what they're doing. A large part of networking is keeping track of what's going on in your field. Networking is a desirable skill to have in any field you work in. Learn how to do it well early in your life, and you'll get ahead.

overcoming your doubts

One of the most important traits a successful actor has is *confidence*. People who get onstage and speak in front of other people, in any business, have found a way to feel they can do the job and do it well. But to get acting jobs, actors have to go through audition after audition. They are turned down so many times for roles that they can form serious doubts about what they're doing. To keep going, they must build a great deal of confidence in themselves. Let's look at some ways to do this.

CONFIDENCE IN YOUR ACTING

To gain the confidence you'll need as a professional actor, you want to make sure you have two things: *good training,* so that you know exactly what you're doing when you begin work on a role, and *experience* in the performing arts. Two or three years of training and another two or three years of experience are the very least you'll need in order to feel comfortable working on a new role. Four or five years of training and the same amount of experience are even better. Quite often, the actors who you see on the big screen completed many years of university and/or professional acting training before they even began their careers, and they may have been gaining experience for many more years, playing role after role.

The more experience you have acting in different kinds of roles, the more confidence and creativity you can bring to your acting.

When you are cast in a role, your experience will have shown you what the process of rehearsal and performance is like. Going into rehearsal for a new show or film is complex. You must get to know the director and the other actors and learn how to work well with them. You must figure out what style the play will have. So you don't want to feel unsure of your skills and abilities as an actor. You want to be free to do the work of creating a character who makes sense within the story the play is telling, rather than trying to figure out *how* to do that.

Occasionally, a young actor who has little training will get a lucky break and get a major role in a play or film. Sometimes that actor can get by on his or her personality and good looks for a while. That actor probably just appears confident and seems to be headed for success. Those are nice traits to start out with, but without the training and experience to know how to create an exciting role time after time, he or she won't be a success for long.

Another way to gain confidence through your acting is to discipline yourself to work, even in the face of the constant rejection that actors experience. In your spare time, work on a monologue to do at auditions, on a character you've been cast to play, or on improving your skills. The more you work on your acting, the more confidence you'll have.

If the audition or opening night arrives and you're not quite sure of your lines, you're adding fear of making a mistake to the nerves that normally occur at these times. But if you know your lines very well, and you're very comfortable in the character's shoes, you'll easily transform the audition or play into an experience of success. Taking the time to do the work well will also strengthen your reputation as a professional.

CONFIDENCE IN YOURSELF

Whether or not anyone has told you that you're a unique and wonderful person, you are. No one else can see things through your eyes. No one else has had exactly the same experiences and thoughts as you have. Each one of us has talents and gifts to give to the world, and you do, too.

Confidence comes from knowing that no matter what you do, or whether you succeed or fail at anything, you still have worth and importance.

TALKING ABOUT ACTING

What part of acting is hardest for you?

Ollie, age 12: *I'm better performing in front of an audience that I don't know at all than in front of my parents and relatives. I'm afraid I might let them down if I mess up.*

A lot of actors feel this way. Yet the people closest to you are the ones who know that even if you make a mistake, you're still the same person they care for. The more you can focus on enjoying the work, and the better prepared you are, the less likely it is that you'll make a mistake or feel bad if something doesn't go exactly right.

Sometimes parents get so busy they forget to teach you to feel good about yourself. Some parents can make you feel bad even though you get good grades and behave well. Some families never learn how to give each other confidence. Some families just have problems.

Every human being on this planet matters. The best thing you can do is trust that you were born for a specific purpose and have something special to give. Then look for ways to live out that purpose.

With the fierce competition in the acting business, there is so much rejection involved that actors sometimes get depressed or despondent about their chances for doing what they love to do. There are support groups for actors who get together once a week or once a month to help each other stay positive—you could find one of these, or check out the Actor's Fund (www.actorsfund.org). If you need a quick boost, look up "confidence" on the Internet and read a few articles. Positive self-help psychology books can also help you to get through some rough spots.

If you ever find yourself feeling unhappy over a long period of time, talk to someone who can truly help you. Life is not meant to be a sad journey through a maze of work and difficulty. There are ways to get back or to build your confidence in your abilities and yourself.

CONFIDENCE IN THE BUSINESS

Confidence in the business comes from knowing how it works. For example, actors feel more sure about what they're doing when they know something about the people they'll audition for. If you're at an interview with an agent, and you can talk about work you enjoyed by one of the agent's successful clients, you'll show him or her that you really know what's going on in the business. If you know who does the casting for this or that theater, you'll know where to send your photo to ask for an audition when a role comes up that you're right for. In other words, knowledge will make you feel confident you can do things to increase your chances of success.

I have mentioned that you'll be turned down for roles—it's a fact of life for actors. Confidence means that you'll understand that rejection is just a part of the business you're in. It is not a rejection of who you are. That's one of the most important things actors must learn about the way show business operates. You are a good and talented and worthwhile person, even if you don't get the roles you want.

You may have to audition many, many times over the course of many years before you begin to be a successful working actor, but you must not take the rejection personally. If you're not chosen for a role, it probably has nothing to do with you or your talent or skill. Perhaps the actor who was chosen already knows the director. Perhaps the choice was based on whether the actor has an accent, or because of the rhythms of his or her speech. Perhaps the director was casting a family and chose actors who had a "family" resemblance to each other. Most of the time, you won't have any idea why someone else was chosen. If you think of it like the lottery, you'll understand that the odds are very high just because so many people are "playing the game." The best thing is just to trust that when the time is right, it will happen for you.

Part of your confidence comes from knowing that it *is* a business, that people are making business decisions when they're casting. In most instances, it's not a matter of playing favorites or picking friends for the kickball game. Although it may feel that way at times, casting choices are generally based on business practices. Sometimes politics influence casting choices, but the dynamics are still based on a business model. Interviewing and auditioning as an actor may stimulate some old memories for you, if you weren't as popular as you wanted to be, or if you were heavily criticized when you were younger. But if you choose acting as a career, you'll need to find ways to help yourself see that it is a business, not a replay of past situations. A good therapist can help you with this, and if you enjoy reading self-help books, that can be another support for you.

Whether or not someone has helped you learn to believe in yourself, confidence is a quality that will help you greatly no matter how the audition turns out. Be confident, and remind yourself after every audition that you're special, even if you don't get the part.

TALKING ABOUT ACTING

How do you feel about auditions?

Chloe, age 15: *I've learned that I'll get really, really nervous if I feel I'm not prepared. But when I'm prepared, I feel confident and do a great job.*

Julie, age 16: *They can be nerve-racking, but if you know what you're doing and you're focused, they can also be fun.*

These are very good points! In an audition, there are many things you can't control, and having the feeling that you'll be judged can in itself make you feel nervous. But if you are confident about your skills, and have mastered the material you'll be presenting, you'll be less nervous because at least you'll know what you're doing at the moment you're presenting your monologue or reading. And when you know what you're doing, you can actually have fun. Don't let the situation or the other actors overrun your focus—keep your attention on yourself and your own work, and be prepared so that you're confident about what you're doing.

There are plenty of old sayings you can repeat to yourself, if that helps:

◆ "That's the way the cookie crumbles!"
◆ "That's life!"
◆ "¡Que sera sera!" (What will be, will be!)

You don't have any control over whether you get cast. But you *do* have control over how you respond to things. The healthy response is to say to yourself, "Oh, well," and forget about that audition and do your best at the next one. If you thought you could have done better at the audition, figure out why and how, and work on fixing that the next time. But don't berate yourself or put yourself down with, "I should have done this or that." Going over and over any negatives you might have noticed will quickly erode your confidence. Focus on fixing a problem if you believe that there is one, and don't hesitate to get help from a teacher or coach.

If you begin to doubt yourself, it's important to overcome the doubts right away. Remember that who you are as a person and the things you *do* control in your life are much more important than whether you got that role. You want to have activities and friendships outside your acting life as well as within it, so you have other things to focus on besides auditions. When you're a well-rounded person with interests of all kinds, you'll be more confident, and you'll be a better performer. When you're happier with your life in general, you'll feel more positive about succeeding in your acting career.

chapter **P**

photos

Photographs are major tools in the actor's task of furthering his or her career. When you've been to a theater, you may have noticed photos of the cast on the bulletin board in the lobby. These are a type of photo called headshots (see Glossary)—and you'll need one of yourself to promote yourself as an actor.

In some smaller towns, you may be able to get started with a good snapshot picture. But offering a Polaroid-type photo to a casting director or agent in a larger city will mark you as a beginner. So it's best to get a set of 8-by-10-inch black-and-white photos as soon as you can. And if you're really serious about acting as a career, you'll need to have the photos taken by a professional photographer for actors. (Color photos are sometimes used for modeling, but the actor's standard is always black and white.)

A session with a good photographer will cost at least $200, depending on how many shots he or she takes. (The type of shots developed will also affect the cost.) The session will take anywhere from one to three hours. The photographer may expect to shoot one roll of film containing thirty-six shots, but if it takes you a while to relax, you'll probably want to have the photographer shoot at least one more roll. If you're planning on getting different types of headshots in the same session, the photographer may take several rolls, and the session will be longer.

TYPES OF HEADSHOTS

Many professional actors get headshots for three different purposes: one for commercials, one for theater, and one for film. At some point early in your career, you'll probably want to have three rolls of shots taken by your photographer—one roll for each type of headshot.

Having three types of headshots means that you can fit your image to what's being cast by choosing the type of photo you send. If you're sending your photo/resume to a casting director who casts television commercials, you want to have an upbeat "smile shot" that shows great energy. A casting director who focuses on commercials probably wouldn't find much value in a serious theatrical headshot. He or she would want to know what you look like when you smile. Similarly, sending in an upbeat smile shot for a role on a soap opera probably wouldn't be as effective as a serious, more theatrical-looking photo.

For a commercial shot, you'd probably want to wear casual clothes, and the photographer would probably suggest relaxed body positions. Remember that agents and casting directors look for a certain energy in a headshot. Most commercial shots are smile shots: the actor is smiling and his or her eyes show energy. These are good shots to do at the beginning of a session when you're fresh and lively. They're difficult to pull off if you're a little tired.

Headshots for theater and film are usually more serious looking. The photographer may suggest dark clothing or a more dramatic style of dress. This is where you can really show your stuff. Be sure to let your eyes reflect energy again—think of your eyes as the windows to your soul, as the saying goes.

FINDING A PHOTOGRAPHER

There may be someone in your hometown who does actors' headshots, but make sure that the person takes black-and-white photos for *actors.* You do not want a portrait-style photo. There are big differences in style and approach between headshots and portraits. If you're really committed to a professional career, it's probably worth a trip to a major city for

CHRIS O'CONNOR

In the standard headshot, like Chris O'Connor's, a natural smile is always a good bet. Notice that Chris has had his name printed at the bottom of the photo.

TANYA OESTERLING

Tanya Oesterling's photo is a good example of the three-quarter shot.

professional headshots if you'll be trying to build your career from some-place else.

If you live in a large city and have the opportunity to choose from several photographers, arrange to meet three or four of them. Look at the work they've done for others and imagine how you'd feel working with each. Just as you get along better with some people than with others, you'll probably find you're more comfortable with one photographer than with another. Each has a unique style: you can probably tell by looking at their work whether you'd like their approach.

When you first talk with the photographer, ask him or her to make some suggestions about your "look." As we've seen, most people in the business categorize actors in their files into types: a young mom or dad, a young romantic lead, a businessperson, and so on. The photographer will have some ideas on this, so ask about type. Check out some actors' photos on the Internet to see what works and what doesn't (see chapter W, "Working the Web," for ideas). If you find something that really strikes you, you could take it in to the session as an example. But remember that you want to be unique, rather than a copy of another actor.

You can ask other actors about photographers they've been to: Were they easy to work with? Did the actor feel he got his money's worth? Some photographers are better than others. Some charge a high price just because they can get it, not necessarily because their work is really good. And there are some photographers for whom picture taking is an art that they love, and it shows through in their photos.

Once you've chosen a photographer, ask about what kinds of clothing you should bring to the photo session. You should plan to dress neatly and comfortably in a way that makes you feel like yourself, for your photos as well as your auditions. Casting directors and agents expect the actors they do business with to look professional, so it's not a good idea to wear sloppy clothes as part of your look.

What do you want from an acting career?

Paula, age 17: *I want success, not in the form of money, but in the form of really great parts. I want it to get even better than I thought it would get.*

This is a very positive perspective. It's good to see success as being not only about making money or achieving fame but about enjoying what you do. But it can be difficult to keep a good balance between having a positive perspective and becoming overly idealistic. If you build your hopes up unrealistically high, you could be in for a long fall if you don't achieve what you want. Professional actors must work hard, audition, and network, even for small roles. The chances to do the great parts are rare. If you start out as too much of a dreamer, you may give up many good things in life for something that might not happen. Then you could feel that life is not "better than you thought it would get," but a bummer. The way to look at it is to focus on reality with a positive attitude.

THE NATURAL YOU

Even though the world of acting appears to be full of glamour and mystery, most agents and casting directors prefer to see a *natural* look in an actor's headshot. It's important to look your best in the photo, but you want to look the way you do on any day you're enjoying life and feeling great—not as if you're getting all done up to go to the Academy Awards. (Even the stars would find it a lot of trouble dressing for the Academy Awards every day.) Most people in the business prefer a fresh, relaxed look in photos. If they need to make you more glamorous for a role, they'll hire hair and makeup professionals.

Most actors use makeup for their photo sessions because the camera picks up every flaw. Your photographer will probably be able to suggest a makeup person for you to work with. Black-and-white photography requires a special knowledge of makeup colors and techniques. So unless you're very experienced, you shouldn't do your own makeup for your photos.

If you study the work of the photographers you visit, you'll be able to see which ones achieve a natural look with makeup in their photos. A good makeup artist can bring your face alive on film, but without giving you a "made-up" look. Be sure to tell the makeup person that you want a natural look rather than a "glam" look. Remember, you need to look just like your photo; otherwise the agent or casting director may become confused about who you are.

CONTACT SHEETS

A few days after the photo session, you'll be able to look at *contact sheets* of your photos. These are groups of very small versions of the shots that were taken. It may seem odd to have so many images of yourself staring back at you. It helps to cut a square out of a piece of paper, about the size of one of the prints, so that you can cover up the remaining images while you look at each one. The images you choose will each be blown up into a headshot. Then you'll go to a photo duplicating service to have more copies made.

As you study the contact sheets, look for a photo in which you look relaxed but energetic. An actor's photo should project a lively quality without overwhelming the viewer. Look for one in which your eyes sparkle, in which you look like you live life fully. If you choose a shot in which you're smiling, make sure the smile looks natural and not forced. Check to make sure there are no funny shadows on your face or distracting elements in the background.

The photographer can help you choose a good photo, and if you know any professional actors, they may give some advice as well. If you're on good terms with others in show business, like an agent, a director, or a casting person, ask them, too. You may choose a shot based on their advice, but be sure that you like the shot, too. You should like the way you look in it, because you'll be using the photo in a lot of different situations for a long time.

COSTS

Photos are one of the biggest investments actors make in their careers. On top of the cost of the photographer, you'll need to spend between $75 and $250 to have copies of your headshots made (depending on how many you start with). There are companies that specialize in making these copies, and they will charge you less than a regular film developer or camera shop. You can ask your photographer about photo duplicating services, or check out ABC Pictures for duplicating (www.abcpictures.com).

As a young actor, you'll probably need to get new headshots every year or two, since you're still growing and changing. Later, every two to four years will be all right as long as your look remains about the same. But if you change your hairstyle, gain or lose more than ten pounds, or have cosmetic surgery, you'll need to get new photos. After all, you want to look just like your headshot when you walk into an audition. If a casting director has called an actor in based on the actor's headshot, the casting director may be a bit confused if the actor shows up with short hair instead of long, or fifteen pounds heavier or lighter. As a professional, you'll need to keep your headshots updated, just as you keep your resume updated.

questions about promoting yourself

If you're planning on an acting career, you'll need to promote yourself using those headshots you just read about. (You'll also need a resume—that's the topic of chapter R.) This chapter provides answers to six questions that are asked over and over again by young actors starting out:

1. How do I get my photo to agents and casting directors?
2. How often should I contact agents and casting directors?
3. Should I take classes with a casting director or agent so that I can meet them?
4. How can I find out what my look or type is?
5. How long should I expect building my career to take?
6. What do I do if I try and try, and nothing happens?

These questions may not sound like matters that your favorite actors would need to think about, but at one time even the biggest stars needed to consider them.

1. How do I get my photo to agents and casting directors? There are two ways to do this. The first is to mail the photo with a resume and cover letter. When you mail a photo, you can follow up a week or so later with a phone call, asking if you might set up a time to come in and interview. The person may be brief with you on the phone, or even rude. Many agents and casting directors prefer to make the first personal contact themselves after they've received an actor's photo. If people seem unkind, remember that it's not because of who you are, or what you want. You may have just caught them at a very busy time, or they may just be rude people!

The second way to get your photo to agents and casting directors is to drop it off in person. Some actors in large cities such as New York and Los Angeles promote themselves this way. But it's very rare that you'll get an interview or audition when you stop by to drop off your photo, and many people in the business prefer not to have actors stop by their office at all without an appointment. Some agents and casting directors are adamant that they *do not* want actors showing up at their offices without an invitation, and if you do so, you'll probably earn their distaste rather than their respect. You may want to meet the people who do the casting and agenting, but they may feel that a total stranger is trying to pressure them if you just walk in.

You can look at the Ross Reports (www.rossreports.com) to find out which casting directors and agents might be amenable to having you drop off your photos in person. If you did decide to visit, you'd want to respect the wishes of the person you visit. If it seems like he or she is in a hurry, just say, "Thank you," and leave. Again, be brief and friendly. Don't try to chat with someone who doesn't seem to want to talk. Don't give someone a reason to remember you in a negative way rather than a positive way.

2. How often should I contact agents and casting directors? Once your photo is in their hands, add their name to your mailing list. Then you'll want to follow up by mailing a flyer or **postcard** every six weeks or so. Using today's computer software, you can print address labels for your cards and flyers from your mailing list, or you can order labels from Henderson Enterprises (www.hendersonenterprises.com) or other such companies. This can make it easier to do your follow-ups on a regular basis—you can simply put the label and a stamp on the back of your post-

Postcard: A postcard-size marketing tool that usually includes one or two of your headshots (reduced), such as a commercial shot and a theatrical shot, and your name and contact information. Postcards cost much less to duplicate and mail than 8-by-10 headshots and help actors to keep in touch in a simple way.

card, write a quick message about your current project or paste on a bit of a good review, and pop it in the mail.

When you're acting in a show, film, or commercial, you will help your career along if you send photo postcards to the people on your mailing list. Be sure to put the information about what you're doing on the reverse side. You can type a small blurb about the show you're doing, or copy a couple of sentences from a great review you received, and cut it out to paste on the back, or write by hand. This is a good way to keep people up to date on how your career is going, and what kinds of roles you're doing. There's always a chance someone will see and take notice of your performance if they have been told about it first. It will also help people see that you are a professional and that you pursue your work seriously.

Also, when you're in a show, you can send a flyer listing the dates, times, and place of performances. If you get a role in a film, send information about the opening of the film and where it will play.

Keep all follow-up messages short, and type or write clearly! Most agents and casting directors receive photos and/or postcards from hundreds of actors every week and don't have time to read long notes or messy writing.

Most actors have to keep contacting and sending messages for months or years before agents and casting directors finally call them. It's your job to keep in touch with them. If they don't reply over a long period of time, you may want to contact a different group of people or change your approach.

3. Should I take classes with casting directors or agents so that I can meet them? There are classes and workshops held by casting directors or agents that are also called "paid auditions." Some actors believe they're a waste of time and money. Other actors have gotten work because of the contacts they made through one of them.

Some of the people who lead these workshops do it only for money. There are others who truly care about helping actors. They see the workshops as a way to meet new talent. A smart actor will ask around to find out if some workshops are better than others.

You can learn a lot about show business, and sometimes about your own type, or get marketing ideas, by attending one of these workshops. If you're curious, try one or two to get a feel for it. Maybe you'll like the way things turn out.

If you've had a particular agent or casting director on your mailing list for a long time, it might be worth taking that person's workshop. Then he or she can meet you in person.

4. How can I find out what my look or type is? One way is to go to as much theater as you can and spend some time watching commercials and television shows. Compare the types of people you see with how you look. You'll get a general idea of where you might fit in. Another resource is a book called *The Player's Guide,* which you may find in major libraries and at offices of the actors' unions. This guide lists actors and actresses *by type.* It is sometimes used by casting directors to cast specific roles. It can help educate you about particular looks and types. In the last few years, *The Player's Guide* has merged with *Showfax,* an online site for actors (www.showfax.com). You can look at other actors' websites and enjoy all kinds of other resources for actors by visiting this site. But if you can find a library copy of *The Player's Guide,* it will give you a lot of understanding about types.

5. How long should I expect it to take to build my career? In a few special cases, actors have begun to work steadily after pursuing a career for only a few years. But most can expect to work on their careers for ten to twenty years before consistently making a living at it. In many cases, actors promote themselves well and make a living doing what they enjoy, but they never find the great success, fame, or money they hoped for. The reasons are usually unknown. It may not be a lack of talent. It may just be timing or luck, or any of a number of reasons. As most actors know, there are many, many talented actors who don't work a lot.

TALKING ABOUT ACTING

What do you think it would be like to be a star?

Quentin, age 14: *I really wouldn't want to be a star. I'd like people to know who I am, but not to the extent of not being able to walk down my own street without people saying, "Oh, look! It's so-and-so!"*

It's easy to see why you feel that way. The lives of stars sometimes seem full of stress and trouble. Many have to hide from reporters or hide from public view. If you don't want to be a star, how would you behave in this profession where stardom does happen to people? It might appear to others that you're sending the message, "I don't really want this"—even at auditions. You might not do your best work. So you must be open to whatever may happen, or you could make choices such as not auditioning for larger roles if you don't want to be a star. It's best to know clearly what you want before you begin.

6. **What do I do if I try and try, and nothing happens?** Remember that it may not be a failure in the way you're promoting yourself or anything else. Don't take the lack of response as a rejection of *you*.

Think about whether you might make some calls to people you've contacted before. Some people need a reminder before they'll agree to see you. It also might help to look at things with a fresh eye. Ask someone you trust for advice. Take a new class. Or get involved in another field in show business—lighting and sound for the stage, camera work for the screen. You'll get a new perspective on the world of show business, and the more you can learn, the better off you'll be.

It's hard to understand sometimes why some actors are successful and others are not. There may be no reason that anyone can see. Some actors pursue a career for a long time without getting the work they wanted. They decide they're not getting as much out of it as they're putting in. At some point, then, they do think about leaving the business. They may quit acting or simply quit trying to make a living at it. They may then act in small theaters, just to enjoy it.

Also, the acting business seems to worship youth and beauty. Actors don't stay young forever, and not everyone is gorgeous. This can make it hard to keep a career going.

But you can always find a place to use your acting talent. Most places you act will not have the pressure that the large cities have.

If you become a professional actor, and eventually find that you feel unhappy with the way your career is going, you can always change your mind and choose another career if you want to. Nothing in life is set in stone. Take some time to make a decision. You might stop acting for a while or continue pursuing an acting career in a different way. Whatever you choose to do, you want to make sure that you're enjoying some part of your life. You want to have activities and friends outside the acting business. You just can't know ahead of time if you'll be successful. If you don't reach your goal, it will be much easier if you've at least enjoyed the ride.

resumes

The resume is one of the actor's most important tools for promoting his or her career. A resume lists the actor's work experience and other information that would interest anyone who would consider him or her for a role. This includes the actor's height, weight, and hair and eye color, and also such things as the range of his or her singing voice and special skills. Let's look at how you can prepare a professional-looking resume to get your own career off the ground.

Your resume should be printed on 8ž -by-11-inch paper and trimmed to 8 by 10 to fit on the back of your headshot. Of course, it must be typed. Casting people usually look at a resume for only a few seconds, so you need to keep your resume on one page and be sure it's clear and easy to read. A confusing or crowded-looking resume will turn people off, so never try to squeeze too much information onto it. As you get more skills and new and better roles, you simply remove the old ones, rather than making the type smaller or more jammed together.

THE FORM OF A RESUME

First of all, your name, telephone number, and email address must be at the top, either in the center or on the left margin. You can find a variety of resume samples on the school websites listed in chapter W, "Working the

Web." It's better not to include your address, because resumes can fall into the hands of people who are up to no good. You never want to advertise where you live.

Many actors pay for an answering service that will take their calls for them. The answering service telephone number is the one they list, not their personal number, so that if their resume happened to fall into unknown hands, someone they didn't know wouldn't be calling them at home. If you can, you should get an answering service also, for the same reason. If you're working with an agent, it's best to list the name of the agency and its phone number, rather than your own.

Cell phones can be very handy for actors, but remember to turn them off when you're in an interview or audition. And as with everything else, remember that they can project an image of you: how you set the ring can influence others' perception of you.

Underneath your name and service or cell phone number on your resume, list your height, weight, hair and eye color, and your **vocal range** if you are a singer. Below this, put in your experience—or credits—for theater, film, and television, in three separate sections. If you're in New York, list your theater credits first; if you're in Los Angeles, list your film credits first. Include the name of the show, the role you played, and the theater at which it was performed. In the case of film and TV, the name of the director or the television network goes in place of the theater name. Put your best credits first, so your best work is the first thing a reader will see. In the example, the actor has no film experience, so she simply lists her theater and TV credits.

> **Vocal range:** This refers to the type of voice you have: bass, baritone, tenor, alto, mezzo-soprano, or soprano. You can find out from a voice teacher, vocal coach, or choir director what type of voice you have, if you don't know offhand. Provide your range on your resume only if you sing very well—casting directors may call you to audition for singing roles.

Actors who have done commercials want to include that experience on their resumes. They should have a copy of the commercial on videotape and state on the resume after the credits: "Videotape available on request."

If you've only begun acting, you may be tempted to "pad" your resume—add credits for shows you haven't actually performed in. This is a no-no! Casting people understand that everyone has to start somewhere, and it's pretty easy for them to spot a resume that's padded. Some casting people have read resumes with phony credits for shows they had cast themselves, so they knew the resumes were false—and threw them away. An actor must build a name as a professional in the business, and that means being honest about what you've done and how you've trained. Nothing turns off a casting person faster than knowing an actor isn't truthful.

The next section of your resume lists your training. Here you can include your acting training and/or classes, voice training, movement or dance classes, and any other training you've gotten. If your acting teacher is fairly well known, you may want to list his or her name—otherwise the school name is fine.

The final section of the resume is a list of the actor's special skills. These can be anything from doing dialects or magic acts to playing sports. Perhaps you do special character voices—such as Arnold Schwarzenegger or Donald Duck. It's important to list only skills that you can do very well. If you list basketball, a casting person may call you to audition for a role because you claim that you can play basketball. You need to be able to perform in an audition "game," and be a pretty good shot, too. If you list fields of interest you know a little about but don't perform well in, you'll mislead casting people. They'll be surprised and not very pleased if they call you in to show them a skill you don't really have.

TALKING ABOUT ACTING

Is there any advice you'd give to other actors?

Rhonda, age 17: *Always be looking for ways to improve your acting. Don't let yourself be average. Never think you are the best you can be—always try to get better.*

Yes, it's important to keep training yourself and improving. But don't tell yourself that you're not good enough, or that most other actors are better. Believe in yourself and your abilities, and at the same time work to be even better.

FINISHING TOUCHES

You can get your resumes copied at most printing or copy shops. If you can afford it, get them copied on a heavy, good-quality paper. Casting people slide resumes in and out of files, so they need to stand up to a lot of shuffling.

Ask for a test sample, or the first copy, and check to make sure it looks straight and centered on the page. When you have your resume copied, ask to have the copies cut to 8 by 10 inches, to match the size of your headshot. Otherwise, you'll have to trim each one yourself to the size of your photo. You don't want the resume to stick out over the edge of the headshot—it will look bad and get torn as it's moved around.

If you have a computer, you can do your resume yourself. Be sure there are no errors—read it carefully, or have someone else proofread it. And use a quality printer with superior paper—remember that your resume is part of your business image.

Your resume must be stapled—at all four corners—or glued to the back of your photo. If your photo and resume are not connected to each other, one may get lost, and the person you give it to will have your photo with no phone number, or your resume with no idea of what you look like.

Every time actors do a new role, they list it on their resumes. When you've had a number of roles, and your resume begins to get crowded, remove some of the less important roles or roles done at less important theaters. Then it will be up to date and still easy to read.

Experienced performers know that the resume is not who they are— it's just the list of their work experiences. When you look at people's resumes, you know they have a life outside that. Your resume doesn't represent the whole of who you are. So when you write your first resume, don't give in to the feeling that you'll never do enough to impress people. Have faith that you are already an interesting person and that you'll fill up the empty spaces on that page with good roles at good theaters as time goes by.

THE COVER LETTER

Whenever you mail out a resume and photo to a casting director or other show-business person, it should have a cover letter (see page 130) attached to it. The cover letter should introduce you and explain in a simple and well-written way why you are contacting the person. If you're currently performing onstage, or a film or television show that you have a good role

Your Name
Street Address
City, State, Zip
Telephone number
Email address

Date

Mickie Johanson
Artists Plus Agency
1201 El Huenga Blvd.
Los Angeles, CA 99999

Dear Ms. Johanson:

I'm new to the Los Angeles Area, and I'd like to introduce myself to you. I recently graduated from Northwestern University, where I performed the roles of Kate in *The Taming of the Shrew*, and Amanda in *Private Lives*, among others.

I'm currently studying with Ralph Hemson at the Studio for Actors, and we'll be presenting an evening of one-acts next month. I'd like to invite you to attend a performance. Enclosed is a fly outlining the dates and times of the shows, along with my photos and resume.

I'd enjoy meeting with you for an interview or audition, at your convenience. Please let me know if you'd like to attend one of the Studio performances, and I'll reserve a complimentary ticket in your name.

Thank you for your consideration.

Sincerely,

[*signature*]

Your name

Enclosure

Your cover letter doesn't have to follow this example exactly, but it is a good guide to what one looks like. Actors who are professional always make sure they spell the name of the person they're writing to correctly. (Notice the name "Mickie"—it's an unusual spelling). People don't like to receive mail with their name spelled wrong!

Which sex is the person if his or her first name is Mickie—or Lynn or Sandy? It could be the name of a male or a female, so you'd need to find out for sure. Finally, you'd check your letter for misspelled words, make it nice to look at, and then paper-clip it to your photo and resume and mail it off.

in will be airing soon, mention that in your cover letter. You can offer to reserve tickets for a show if you're writing to a casting person or agent. If you have a video of your work, you can mention that in your letter. If you have a request, such as inquiring about an interview, make it brief and to the point.

Of course, the cover letter, like the resume, must always be neatly typed, for two reasons: First, it looks much more professional. And second, some people don't want to read handwriting, even if your handwriting's terrific. Remember, too, that casting people and agents are busy, so keep the letter brief and clear.

In the next chapter, you'll find out how to keep your spirits up while you're promoting yourself as an actor.

self-esteem

You've already seen how important it is for an actor to be confident. No actor wants to go on the stage or in front of a camera feeling uncertain about himself or what he's doing. Actors need to feel sure of their acting skills and abilities. But they also need to respect themselves as human beings and artists and learn how to take care of their own needs. They need what is called *self-esteem.*

There's a big difference between truly feeling good about yourself and *pretending* to be confident. Some people grow up with a healthy sense of self-esteem—they believe strongly in themselves and their abilities, and they generally feel good about who they are and what they're doing. They can easily work toward and achieve what they want in their lives. Others are somewhat shy and feel more unsure of themselves or think of themselves as unworthy of respect and success. A person's sense of self-esteem is often based on childhood experiences with family or schoolmates.

Some people *appear* to be sure of themselves all the time. They never seem to make a mistake, causing others to wish they could be as "together" as that person. But sometimes their appearance can be a cover-up for other kinds of feelings—a fear of seeming foolish, or confused, or boring—in other words, a feeling that there is something wrong with them. Sometimes the biggest egotist feels really small inside.

People who have a lack of self-esteem often have trouble dealing with others in a healthy way. People who pretend to be perfect are usually quite afraid of making a mistake or of doing something to offend other people. Their air of confidence is just a mask.

You may meet some people during your career who are faking it. They will boast about this or that role or talk about all the famous people they have worked with. But sometimes you can't tell it's a bluff. Some actors—and even agents, directors, and producers—are good at making things up about their experiences and careers. Trust your instincts: if you feel funny about a particular person or situation, you're probably right—there may be a hidden agenda. If you associate more with people who are truly confident, your own self-esteem will grow.

WHAT IS SELF-ESTEEM ALL ABOUT?

Actors have a lot to offer their friends, family, and the people who come to see them perform. That's what makes most actors feel good about themselves. It gives them a sense of their worth, whether they make it on Broadway or act in a community theater in the smallest town in Iowa. That's self-esteem.

Having self-esteem doesn't mean that you have to feel sure of yourself all the time. Healthy self-esteem means that you care for yourself and believe in yourself even if you make a mistake or fail at something you try to do. Mistakes and failures are simply part of the human experience, and it's important for an actor to be human. That makes people want to watch you.

TALKING ABOUT ACTING

What do you think would be the hardest part of being a professional actor?

Ajala, age 16: *Commitment to that and not to your life.*

This is one of the misunderstandings that can cause actors to become depressed if they struggle for years without much success, or if their careers haven't turned out the way they had hoped. Many actors make the mistake of putting all of their time and energy into their careers, leaving none for their life. Then over time, they become dependent on getting cast to feel like there's something worth living for. And if they don't get to perform as much as they want to, they sometimes end up feeling that life isn't really worth living between roles. I've known a number of actors who have gone into the business with this perspective. It always creates disappointment down the road, and it usually means that the actor has to spend a lot of time and energy at some point learning how to reinvest herself in her life. It would be much better to decide at the beginning to commit to your life first and your career second. Then if your career doesn't work out the way you expected, you already have a rich life, and it's not nearly as disappointing.

We've already talked about how important training is. As many actors pursue their careers, they continue to take classes of some kind to stay confident in their skills. This keeps their belief in themselves strong. When you're not working as an actor, it's easy for your self-esteem to slide. And since you may not get steady work as an actor in the first few years of your career, you'll need to find ways to keep building your self-esteem.

One way to build confidence in your work is to focus on what you do well, rather than on things you did poorly. If you work to improve in areas where you feel you're lacking, that will also build your confidence. If you feel like you blew it at an audition, remember all the other auditions you felt good about. Even if you weren't cast, you've done work you can be proud of—and you can do great work in the future.

It's also important to notice the other things that you do well outside of acting: Are you an excellent cook? A really good friend? Are you very competent when you work at your day job? Reminding yourself that you are very capable and skilled in other areas of your life besides acting will help to build your confidence. Good self-esteem comes from knowing that you are a valuable person whether or not you get the role you want, whether or not you achieve the success you hope for.

Rather than dwell on mistakes they have made, actors need to put their attention on what they do well. There are other auditions to come. But starting out in an acting career, it's sometimes very hard to feel good about yourself. You may audition for a role that you've always wanted to play, but then not get cast. It's easy to feel you'll never have another chance or that you'll never make it. Many actors have become deeply depressed about losing a role they dreamed of playing. The problem with this is that it gets in the way when they go to the next audition. Their sadness or anger shows through, and their work isn't as good as it could be. If they get stuck in their troubled feelings, the problem just gets worse.

If this happens to you, the best way out would be to see that you're just having a bad time right now and that things will get better. As one actor said, "I feel so low, there's nowhere to go but up." The Actors' Fund (www.actorsfund.org), an organization that helps actors, offers free or low-cost "crisis counseling," opportunities to find work outside of the acting business, and other aid programs for actors. If you get into a depression that lasted for more than a few weeks, it would be helpful to call the Actors' Fund or see a counselor or therapist. If you're in any kind of situation where someone is making you feel bad, or you feel like you can't do anything right, you may need some help getting out of the situation. The Actor's Fund exists to give you a hand with that. If you have financial trouble that is pulling you down, check out the Actors Work Program (www.actorsfund.org/services/Sideline_Work_and_New_Careers/Actors_Work_Program/index_html). It never hurts to ask for help if things seem overwhelming—people at these programs are very understanding.

TALKING ABOUT ACTING

What's your favorite thing about acting?

Yvonne, age 16: *The best thing about being on stage is that for a short time my imagination takes hold, and I can be so many different things that, in reality, I could never even think about. But you can be those things in reality, because they come out of your own imagination. You don't have to be acting to be clever, or strong, or smart, or whatever quality it is that you love about the character you're playing. You already have those wonderful qualities inside of yourself, whether you're acting or not. Allowing yourself to acknowledge and express all that you have inside means you have self-esteem.*

FEELINGS AND SELF-ESTEEM

Some people choose an acting career because it offers an opportunity to express their feelings. Having strong feelings can make us feel out of control, "out there," even naked. It can be difficult to express feelings in social or work situations. For this reason, you may feel like saving up all your feelings for your acting work, allowing your acting to become your only emotional outlet. But this can cause difficulties later on—if you decide to leave the acting business, or if you don't get roles as often as you expect to, you won't have any way to express your feelings.

Feelings are a normal part of human life, and if you can find ways to express them outside your acting, and tell yourself it's okay to do this, you'll get used to sharing your feelings with others. And that's good—as you do this more and more in your day-to-day life, your self-esteem will grow. Let's think about how this works.

Our society isn't used to seeing people express feelings in everyday life. So people who have strong feelings, but don't see other people expressing them, may simply think that nobody else has feelings like theirs. They may then try to deny their feelings or try to cover them up (or wait to express them while performing a role, if they're actors). But once someone shares feelings, he or she usually finds out that other people have just the same kinds of feelings. It's just that they're covering them up, too, for the same reasons.

Some families have a kind of "code" that requires family members to shut off or hide their feelings, but this is not really healthy. It's best to try sharing your feelings at first with someone you really trust—a close friend or an understanding family member. As you become more comfortable with sharing your emotions, thoughts, and beliefs with others, you'll become more confident that the person you are inside is valuable and important, no matter what you feel.

PLANNING AND SETTING GOALS
CAN HELP SELF-ESTEEM GROW

Planning and goal setting are not much fun for most people. But they're important in terms of keeping yourself and your life on track. If you were to move to New York City in one jump, without making any plans, and without knowing anyone there, and without saving some money first, your first few weeks in the city would probably be a shock. It would take a long time to regain your balance.

Such a move would be a blow to anyone's self-esteem. But if you planned your move over a period of several months, and knew exactly where you would stay, and had a plan for finding work, and had enough money to last you for a while, you could make the move with confidence.

It works the same way with a career—any career. If you have a plan for how to build your career, you'll be more likely to succeed. If you have goals for your life, you'll be more likely to achieve what you want to. Don't just let things happen to you and then try to deal with them—that's a pretty hard way to move toward getting what you want, and it can make you feel like you have no control.

TALKING ABOUT ACTING

What are you looking for in an acting career?

Sam, age 18: *I would be doing it for the credit. A lot of actors don't become well known, but people who are in the business know them well. I'd like to have a real name in the theater community and be respected.*

This is a more realistic goal than "I want to be a star" or "I want to be rich." It's a goal you have more power to achieve. For instance, you can get solid training in a good program, work hard, and always be prepared. Then others in show business will respect you. For that kind of goal, there are actual steps you can take to get there.

Setting goals is a part of planning that a lot of people have trouble with. Many young actors set goals such as "I'm going to be a star," or "I'm going to be on Broadway in five years." These are not bad goals to have, but the problem with goals like these is that you have no clear way to work toward them.

Setting a goal is the first step in making a dream come true. But you need to choose words that make it clear that you can actually achieve the goal *all by yourself*. This is what will build your self-esteem and sense of accomplishment. For example:

> "I will send my photo and resume to every casting director that casts on Broadway this year. I will call each one two weeks after I send the photos and ask for an interview."

See? This way, you actually have the power to achieve your goal. You have clearly outlined steps to take, and you can see your progress clearly. So when you have finished, you can tell yourself, "I chose to do that, and I did it. I was successful."

If you choose "I'm going to be on Broadway within five years" as a goal, there are a lot of steps you can take to try to reach it. But in the end there are too many things you can't control:

◆ Which shows are chosen (you may not happen to be right for any of the roles)
◆ Whether another actor has a stronger contact with the casting person (and gets the role because of that)
◆ Whether the director thinks you're just the actor for the part (he or she may want someone who is taller or shorter, stockier or thinner, etc.)

It's very helpful to write your goals down, for several reasons: one is that the process of coming up with the exact words you want to write helps you to get specific about your goal. Another is that you can refer back to your goal(s) over time, to remind yourself what you're working toward, and to check on your progress. Putting your goals in writing also makes them more concrete so that they're not floating around in your head subject to changes in your mood or state of mind.

TALKING ABOUT ACTING

What do you think it would be like to be a professional actor?

Serena, age 15: *I think it would be extremely difficult. It's a high-stress occupation that pays very little, but from what I've done and heard, it's worth it.*

If acting is what you live for, if your life would be empty without it, then you may want to give a career a try. Just don't forget that there may be easier ways to get what you want: by acting in community theater or exploring the arts in other ways. There are many, many possibilities in life, so don't narrow yourself to the "I have to be a star" mentality. That can cut you off from a lot of excitement in other parts of your life.

When there are many things that you can't control, you don't have the power to achieve your goal on your own without getting lucky—and that can make you feel helpless or powerless. And you can't count on luck. It's much better for an actor's self-esteem to have some goals you can be sure of achieving on your own. It's also important to have goals in your life outside of acting. If it turns out that you're not as successful with your career as you'd like to be, you'll still have good self-esteem because you know that you can succeed in other areas of your life.

An actor's life can be full of ups and downs. It's easy to feel that there's too much information to learn and too much work to do, so it's important to do those other things that make you feel good about yourself.

Keep your self-esteem going, and make it a point every day to do one thing you do very well—cooking, making music, dancing, talking politics—whatever it may be. And remember that whatever happens, you have gifts to offer to the world. No one can take away your relationship with yourself. Believe in yourself, and others will, too.

39 plays to be familiar with

ertain plays and musicals are done often at colleges, high schools, regional and summer stock theaters, and community theaters. Whether you're a beginning or more experienced actor, you need to read as many plays as you can, and these thirty-nine plays are good ones to begin with. Many of them call for young actors, and you can often find several of them together in a compilation of classic plays.

TALKING ABOUT ACTING

What do you think would be the hardest thing about being a professional actor?

Tonda, age 14: *Just getting parts. Going to audition after audition, and getting turned down 99 percent of the time.*

That's a pretty hard thing, since it can go on for years and years that way. You need a deep love for the art of acting and fierce commitment to keep at it when the odds are so tough.

Thirty-nine may seem like a lot, but if you're serious about a career, you'll want to read plays until you're familiar with many more than that. Don't feel you have to know all of these plays before you become an actor or read them all within a few weeks. But do keep reading. For starters, spend an afternoon browsing at the library and choose a couple that appeal to you. Choose different types of plays to read. The more you read, the more you'll learn about the different styles that dramatists use to tell a story and bring their characters to life.

Often, when an audition for a particular play is announced, you can get a copy of the script to read at the library or a local bookstore. Of course there are many, many more plays that are well written and often performed; this listing is just to give you a basic grounding in different types of plays.

Remember, your goal is just to become familiar, as professional actors are, with different types and styles of plays. These thirty-nine plays are listed in alphabetical order, not in order of importance. Also included is a list of musicals that are often performed, for those who are interested in that popular form of theater. Titles marked with an asterisk (*) are especially good for beginning and younger actors.

CLASSIC PLAYS

Hamlet, and many others by William Shakespeare
The Cherry Orchard, by Anton Chekhov
The Children's Hour, by Lillian Hellman
The Crucible, by Arthur Miller
Cyrano de Bergerac, by Edmund Rostand
* *The Diary of Anne Frank,* by Albert Hackett and Frances Goodrich
A Doll's House, by Henrik Ibsen
The Glass Menagerie, by Tennessee Williams
* *I Remember Mama,* by John Van Druten
The Importance of Being Earnest, by Oscar Wilde
The Member of the Wedding, by Carson McCullers
The Miracle Worker, by William Gibson
The Miser, by Moliere
* *Our Town,* by Thornton Wilder
Tea and Sympathy, by Robert Anderson
Waiting for Godot, by Samuel Beckett

Young actors find good roles in the play *The Diary of Anne Frank*. For this reason it is often performed in high schools and colleges.

PLAYS OF OUR TIME

Anna in the Tropics, by Nilo Cruz
Brighton Beach Memoirs, and others by Neil Simon
Crimes of the Heart, by Beth Henley
Equus, by Peter Shaffer
Hatful of Rain, by Michael V. Gazzo
The Heidi Chronicles, by Wendy Wasserstein
Intimate Apparel, by Lynn Nottage
Joe Turner's Come and Gone, and others by August Wilson
A Life in the Theater, by David Mamet
Play It Again, Sam, by Woody Allen
Topdog/Underdog, by Suzan-Lori Parks
The Zoo Story, by Edward Albee

All the plays above are comedies and dramas and are most likely shelved in your library under the author's name. Musicals, which are listed next, are usually shelved differently, and you would probably find them arranged by title.

TALKING ABOUT ACTING

Do you have any advice for beginning actors?

Ryan, age 16: *No matter what part you are cast in, never let it get you down. The roles that I didn't want are actually the ones I've had the most fun with.*

That's a good realization! Sometimes, when you're cast in a role that doesn't mean as much as one you really want, you're freer to take risks and have fun. If it's a small role, it gives you the chance to explore tremendously in rehearsal, because you're not so busy learning lines and blocking. Use these opportunities to work on your craft. How much detail can you put into each moment? Can you make some riskier choices with the five lines you have? With your characterization? Look at smaller or less attractive roles as an opportunity to stretch yourself in new ways.

MUSICALS

* *Annie*
  Carousel
* *The Fantasticks*
* *Fiddler on the Roof*
  Guys and Dolls
  Gypsy
  Oklahoma!
* *Oliver!*
* *Peter Pan*
* *The Sound of Music*
* *You're a Good Man, Charlie Brown*

Also, don't forget that many libraries now allow you to check out recordings, videotapes, or DVDs of many of these shows. Have fun reading and exploring!

unions for actors

The unions that you have read about in this book are organizations that protect actors on the job, helping them get fair payment and work under reasonable conditions. Most professional actors belong to at least one of the unions. All actors should respect what the unions do to help performers.

The major role of the unions is to make sure actors are paid a fair amount for their work. That is, they protect *minimum rates* of payment to performers. They also limit the number of hours actors can be asked to work, and they aid actors who have trouble getting paid. Some unions also provide medical and dental benefits, retirement plans, casting information, and other services.

These are the unions for performers:

◆ Actors' Equity Association (also known as AEA, or Equity) covers work in theaters.
◆ American Federation of Television and Radio Artists (AFTRA) covers work in television and radio.
◆ American Guild of Musical Artists (AGMA) members are singers, dancers, and other performers in operas, musical productions, and concerts.

- American Guild of Variety Artists (AGVA) members work in ice shows, nightclubs, theme parks, cabarets, and variety shows.
- Screen Actors Guild (SAG) covers films, TV shows, and commercials.
- Screen Extras Guild (SEG) covers background or extra players for film and TV.

Each union has its own set of requirements for becoming a member. They all require performers to pay fees to join and charge yearly dues. Most of the membership fees (paid when you first join) range from $800 to $1,000. Yearly dues usually run around $40 to $60 for each union.

If you are a member of one union, your dues for a second one, if you want to join another one, will usually be reduced. The first union you joined then becomes your "parent union."

TALKING ABOUT ACTING

Will you be pursuing a professional career?

Uma, age 16: *If I think I'm ready for it. College will be more competitive than high school—and that's the way it'll be on Broadway. So if I feel I can keep up in college, I might try New York. But if I don't think I can, I'll just get another job and do community theater. Then you still get to act, and you kind of get a name and meet lots of nice people.*

That's an excellent way to find out if you want to pursue an acting career. In high school and college, you'll find out if you're comfortable with competition and get a feel for the kinds of roles you'd be cast in. Even if you win the best roles, it doesn't mean you'll always get good ones or be a star later. Theater in New York and the rest of the world will be very different from your school experiences. There will be actors with more skill and experience who've been around longer than you have, and casting directors will be looking for "types" more often than not. So training is important not only to give you a good skill base, but it will also help you figure out if a professional career is right for you.

FACTS ABOUT UNIONS

Many actors think that if they can just get a union membership card, they'll be seen as professionals and consequently have a better chance at getting cast. This idea is a myth. First of all, being a professional means that you have the skills and experience necessary to do the job well, just as you would if you were working in another field. It's not a position or status that suddenly gets you to the top. Professional status is a reputation that's built over time as an actor works with a lot of people. It shows up in your behavior and includes being on time, learning your lines, not missing entrances, being prepared, and having the skills you need to do your job well. Being a professional also means that you've developed your talent and skill to a very high level, which takes time and attention.

It's true, some casting directors and agents will take a different view of you if you have a union card. But most can tell whether your membership in the union is based on the experience and skill they expect from a union member or whether you just paid money for the union card so you could put it on your resume.

Also, once you join a union you'll be competing against thousands of other actors who have already spent a lot of time and gained a lot of experience in the business. If you're a new Equity member, and you audition for your first off-Broadway play, there will probably be actors there who have performed in many plays on and off-Broadway. Quite a few will probably already know the director, and some will already have worked with him or her. Once you join a union, you are in a bigger group of very fine actors who are competing with you for roles. And if you don't know some of the directors, producers, and casting people who will audition you, you'll have a lot of new ground to cover, compared to those who have many more years of experience.

The other thing to keep in mind about unions is that once you are a member, you cannot take nonunion jobs. For example, if you become a member of Equity, you can't work in an off-off-Broadway play that has not agreed to follow union rules. If you become a member of SAG, this means you can't work in a nonunion film. It's very important to get as much experience—and as many credits for your resume—in nonunion venues as you can before competing with more experienced actors. One advantage of waiting to get your union card is that every year there seem to be more and more nonunion films that make it big.

Once in a while an actor secretly appears in a nonunion production when he or she is a union member, but this idea is looked down on in the business. It's not professional behavior.

So, when you become a union member you can lose chances to get hired in some of the places where actors often start out. It's best to wait to join a union until you have solid experience and have been networking for a number of years.

Yet it can be helpful to join a union when the time is right. Most unions have workshops and programs which can help you build your career. For instance, AFTRA often holds meetings with invited agents and casting directors. These kinds of meetings can give you a lot of information about what agents and casting directors are looking for and what kinds of actors they like to work with and can improve your understanding of the business. SAG also has workshops for its members.

If you become a union member and go to these workshops, you'll still want solid training and experience behind you. It's not much help meeting a casting director or agent if you haven't done much acting. People in the business will not often take a risk with a newcomer. So "pay your dues"—get good training and start building a career—before you pay your dues as a union member. You'll increase your chances of success.

videos

Videos are another important tool that actors use to promote themselves, although a video is not a necessity early in your career the way a photo and resume is. In fact, for a beginning actor, spending time and money on a video is usually a waste of both and can even be detrimental to your career down the road if your performance shows that you don't have much experience. Once you have gained good experience working in front of a camera, then you can invest in a video that will show you at your best—sending one out that does otherwise can do more harm than good to your career.

The actor's video usually consists of a few film scenes or commercials in which you have several lines or a leading role, edited together into a five- to seven-minute video. Once you've put the video together, you can also include it on your web site, if you have one. Creating your own personal site for acting allows casting directors and agents to find out more about you than they can learn by looking at your photo and resume, and gives you a chance to be more creative in your self-promotion. Read more about creating your own site in the next chapter, "Working the Web."

If you haven't yet worked on any films or commercials in which you have lines, you can work on a scene with another actor and use that. But it's very important to put only high-quality work on your video. It's a part of the professional image you present, just like your photo and resume.

The scene should be rehearsed well, and the camera work and editing should be done by a professional.

If you're just starting out as an actor, look for auditions for student films—the movies made by students in filmmaking programs at New York University, UCLA, and other schools. Films made by junior and senior students are usually of better quality and may be fine to include in your video. You can find out about the auditions for student films in the weekly theater newspapers like *Back Stage*. Often the auditions are also posted on the bulletin boards of the schools. Student films can be an excellent way to gain experience and credits performing on film.

HOW TO PUT A VIDEO TOGETHER

Let's say you're an actor who has done quite a bit of film work and several commercials. On each job, you've asked the director or the casting person how to get a copy of your work on tape. Once you've collected some of the tapes, look in the yellow pages to find out who does professional editing in your area, or call one of the unions to ask for advice on getting your video professionally edited. It's much better if you can find an editor who has already done videos for actors. He or she will already know what is needed.

Consider choosing scenes that present a fairly consistent image of you, or have them edited in a way that creates a nice flow. A video that begins with a comedy sketch, moves into a graphic death scene in a film, and finishes with a commercial for diapers could be unsettling for a casting person to watch. You want to leave them with not only an idea of the variety of work you can do but a feeling for the "essence" of you that comes across in your acting. This can be related to look or type but should be somewhat consistent.

The editor will help you decide how to edit your scenes together so they present you well. Remember, you are promoting yourself, so you want to focus on your image—how you look and how you come across—because on a video that's what will have the most effect on people watching it. He or she will also help you create titles to introduce each different part of the video. Your name and contact information should be seen at the beginning and end of the video.

If you have some very contrasting film on yourself, you might consider making two tapes, just as actors have different headshots for commercials and for film. One video could include commercials and lighter scenes; the other could include more serious TV and film work. Then you could choose which to send to each casting person based on the type of casting they do. This would especially be a good idea after you've pursued your career for many years and have some good film to show. Sometimes it's helpful to limit the scope of your varied skills and styles on a video because it can make it easier for a casting person to "file" you, both in their heads and in their files. Too much variety or too many possibilities can be confusing.

Editing time in a studio can be expensive, so ahead of time, if you can, choose which scenes you want to put on tape. Also think about the order you may want to put them in. You probably love all the work that you've done, but in choosing what to put on a video, it's helpful to get advice from other professionals in the acting business (just as you do when looking at contact sheets from your headshot photographer). It's hard to look at your own work with an objective eye, and what you may think is a great scene may not impress someone else. If you know any actors who have been pretty successful in the business, you might invite them to watch your scenes and ask them which ones might be best to put on a video. Even better, if you know a teacher or director who might be willing to do this, ask for his or her help.

Once you've had your tape edited, you'll need to get copies made. You always want to have some ready to give to casting people or agents. *Never* send out the original! If it ever gets lost, you'll have to start all over again. The video editor may be able to tell you where you can get copies made at a fair price.

Have your name and contact information printed on both the tape itself and the box it's stored in. No one should need to watch the tape just to find out whose it is. You can make your own labels on a word processor or computer and paste them on the tape and box. You can also paste one of your photo postcards on the box—that's a good example of putting a package together to promote yourself as an actor.

What do you want from an acting career?

Vince, age 13: *I just want a career! It would be a dream come true to be able to have a steady acting job, preferably on the stage.*

The important thing is to keep up that enthusiasm for your dream, even while you're doing the work of building a career. If you can keep reaching for the dream, and believing in it, but also understand the work it will take, your realism will help you succeed.

FILMING YOUR OWN SCENES

If you're a member of SAG or AFTRA, you may be able to use the union's services to film your own scenes for a video. Again, you must make sure that the work you do, and the filming of the scene, looks professional.

Choose a scene that allows you to express some of your range as an actor, but keep it natural as well. You may think that if you only have five to seven minutes to show your talent, you should try to squeeze every possible emotion into the scene. But simpler is better, especially on film. You want to get casting people and agents interested in seeing more of what you can do—not to put the video away thinking they've seen everything you've got.

For your scene partner, choose an actor who is on your own level of skill but is not the same type as you are. It should be someone that you enjoy working with. If you can, find a scene that has humor as well as emotion—everyone likes to laugh. And have fun with the scene, so that when people see the video, they'll enjoy your work even more. If there's a director or acting teacher that you have a good relationship with and enjoy working with, ask him or her for help in putting the scene together.

GETTING YOUR VIDEO
TO CASTING PEOPLE AND AGENTS

Most casting people and agents do not want to get videos they haven't asked for, so it's not a good idea just to mail yours out to them without an invitation. You need to make a contact with someone and make sure it's okay before you send your video. If you send out unrequested videos, they may even just get thrown away.

When you send your photo and resume to a casting person or agent, you can mention in your cover letter that you have a video and would be happy to drop it by or send it to them. If an agent has called you in for an interview, you can take a copy of your video along, then ask during the interview if the agent would like to see it. He or she may ask you to leave it. That gives you the chance to call the agent in a week or two. When you call, ask if the agent got a chance to watch it and when you might pick it up. When you work with an agent, he or she may want to keep a copy of the video to show to a casting person or producer.

Keep track of your video copies the way you keep track of how many photos and resumes you have "out there." Don't let your supply get too low. If you get a chance to send or drop off a video, you want to have one ready—not make the person wait a week while you get copies made.

And keep track of who has seen your video. If you ask someone if he'd like to see your video, and he's already seen it, you'll look a little silly.

It may seem like you have to put a lot of time, energy, and money into creating a video. But the more professional it looks, the more likely it is that you'll be called in for an audition or interview by someone who sees it. Remember to update your video—it's like updating your resume. When you've done a few new films or commercials, have your video redone so that it presents your work as you improve as an actor.

chapter **W**

working the web

If you're like most people, you look to the Internet for information, ideas, and possibilities. This chapter will give you some tips on websites related to acting and the business that can help you get started in this area.

A word of warning: even though the web can inform and inspire you, there are still folks out there who want to make a quick buck and think that actors are easy targets. Some of the sites that offer to post your photo and resume for a fee may not necessarily be worth the money you spend. Casting directors and agents already have access to a large pool of actors whose work they've seen, and who have professional credits. It's not likely that they will be searching the web for actors, unless there is a very unusual role to fill, or they've heard about you somewhere else. Posting your photo and resume on all the sites for actors doesn't guarantee that you'll be noticed, and there is such a thing as overkill.

A better idea, if you can spend some money or have some time, is to put up your own web page and/or blog with your photo, resume, a gallery of images such as character shots or photos from shows, film clips, and information about yourself. That way, you can include the web address on your resume, and refer new contacts to your web page. You can even send email updates which include images and sound clips, rather than paying for postcards and postage. If you're a beginning actor, you probably want to wait until you have some recognized roles on your resume before you put yourself out there.

Although the website doesn't need to be professionally designed, it should be professional looking. Photos of pets, vacations, and the like aren't really appropriate. Remember that you are presenting yourself as a businessperson as well as an actor. Make the site easy to navigate and use—casting directors and agents are busy people, and if your site takes a lot of time to load, or if visitors have to click through several pages to get the information they're looking for, they'll move on to something else. Check out some other actors' sites to get ideas (see the section on Showfax below).

If you decide to hire a web designer for the site, find out whether he or she has created sites for actors, and make sure you check out examples before you sign any kind of agreement. Look for designers through another site that you trust, such as www.backstage.com—this way you're getting a referral to someone with whom others have had a good experience.

Following are more good ways for actors to use the Internet.

RESEARCH THEATER TRAINING PROGRAMS
(see also chapter L, "Learning Your Craft")

The web provides a wonderful resource for research—where you used to have to call or write for a brochure or other information, you can now find practically everything you want to know at your fingertips. Following is a list of well-regarded theater training programs, ranging from certificate programs to undergraduate and MFA programs; you can visit their sites to find out exactly what each offers.

American Academy of Dramatic Arts
www.aada.org

American Conservatory Theater,
    the ACT Conservatory
www.act-sfbay.org/conservatory/
    index.html

Boston University, Theatre Arts
www.bu.edu/cfa/theatre/index.htm

Brandeis University, Theater Arts
www.brandeis.edu/theater/

California Institute of the Arts School
of Theater
www.calarts.edu/schools/theater/index
.html

Carnegie Mellon University School
of Drama
www.cmu.edu/cfa/drama/

CAST Academy of Acting and
Showcase Theater
(Minneapolis, MN)
www.actortrainingcast.com

Columbia University
wwwapp.cc.columbia.edu/art/app/arts/
theatre/index.jsp

DePaul University Theatre School
http://theatreschool.depaul.edu/

Florida State University School
of Theatre
http://theatre.fsu.edu/

Indiana University, Bloomington,
Department of Theatre & Drama
www.indiana.edu/~thtr/index.html

The Juilliard School
www.juilliard.edu

LAMDA, London Academy of Music
and Dramatic Art, Drama School
www.lamda.org.uk/front_content.htm

New York University Tisch School of
the Arts
www.tisch.nyu.edu/page/home

North Carolina School of the Arts
www.ncarts.edu/ncsaprod/drama/

Northwestern University, Weinberg
College of Arts and Sciences
www.communication.northwestern
.edu/theatre/undergraduate/

Penn State University, Theatre Arts
www.theatre.psu.edu

RADA, Royal Academy of Dramatic
Art
www.rada.org

SUNY Purchase
www.purchase.edu/Departments/
AcademicPrograms/Arts/TAF/

Southern Methodist University,
Meadows School of the Arts,
Division of Theatre
http://meadows.smu.edu

Temple University Department of
Theater
www.temple.edu/theater

UCLA Department of Theater
www.tft.ucla.edu/

USC School of Theatre
http://theatre.usc.edu

University of California, Irvine,
    Department of Drama
http://drama.arts.uci.edu/

University of California, San Diego,
    Department of Theatre and Dance
www-theatre.ucsd.edu

University of Delaware, Professional
    Theatre Training Program
www.udel.edu/theatre

University of Illinois,
    Urbana–Champaign, Department
    of Theatre
www.music.uiuc.edu/theatre

University of Iowa, Department of
    Theatre Arts
www.uiowa.edu/~theatre

University of Missouri, Kansas City,
    Theatre Department
http://iml.umkc.edu/theater/

University of Texas, Austin,
    Department of Theatre & Dance
www.utexas.edu/cofa/theatre

University of Washington, School of
    Drama
http://depts.washington.edu/uwdrama/

Yale School of Drama
www.yale.edu/drama

OTHER WEBSITES RELATED TO TRAINING

(see descriptions in chapter L, "Learning Your Craft")

National Foundation for Advancement
    in the Arts: www.nfaa.org
Magnet high school programs:
    www.magnet.edu
The National Association of Schools of
    Theater: http://nast.arts-
    accredit.org/index.jsp

Stage Door Manor Theater Summer
    Camp: www.stagedoormanor.com
Walden Theatre, Louisville, KY:
    www.waldentheatre.org
The University/Resident Theatre
    Association: www.urta.com

SITES TO GIVE YOU A HAND

One of the most difficult aspects of being a professional actor is consistently keeping in touch with your network. Deborah Corbin, an
actress herself, started an Internet business known as ActorMail

(www.actormail.com) to help actors with the tedious task of keeping in touch. Once you've registered, you can arrange to have your photos mailed either when you choose—i.e., you provide ActorMail with a list of names and addresses to which you'd like your information mailed—or you can keep a number of photos on file with them, and when you see a casting notice you'd like to submit to, simply call ActorMail and they'll mail it out that day.

Some sites you might come upon if you search on the net for "casting" will require a fee. It's up to you, the businessperson, to find out whether these sites really offer information or connections that are worth the fee.

If you prefer to mail your photos yourself, or if you're at a stage in your career where you can't yet afford to have someone else "do all the work," check out Henderson Enterprises at www.hendersonenterprises.com. This company provides preprinted labels addressed to casting directors, agents, personal managers, theater companies, and more, as well as guides to people in the business and books for actors (click on Books/Publications). This is a great site to visit to get a feeling for what the business aspect of show business is all about. Label sets are not overly expensive and can save you lots of time—instead of typing addresses on your own labels, you just add a pre-printed one to address your envelope.

When you're getting ready to put your promotion package together, one site where you can find out about getting reproductions of your headshot and photo postcards is www.abcpictures.com. ABC offers full reproduction services at good prices, and once you have your photo in a digital file with them, ordering is quick and easy. The site offers models of available photo and postcard styles, and you can order a free catalog and samples. ABC also provides posters, business cards, and color photos for modeling.

TALKING ABOUT ACTING

What advice would you give to other young actors?

Wally, age 21: *Never forget who you are! It's easy to lose yourself in a role— I've done it many times. You have to keep a grip on reality. Sometimes it's hard to come out of the fairy tale, but you have to.*

Every so often, take stock of where you are and where you're going, in every area of your life. It's easy to get wrapped up in your career or to get going on automatic pilot and to lose a sense of who you are and what you want. Then it's time to step back and think about what's best for you. If you ever felt you could be losing your grip, stop and talk to someone you trust—a family member or friend or counselor. You need to love yourself whether you achieve the success you want or not. When you take care of yourself—your body, mind, and spirit—it shows in your acting and in your relationships with people both in and outside the business.

As you go about the business of keeping in touch, you need to keep your contact information updated. Sites for theatrical publications include *Back Stage*, the theatrical weekly in New York and L.A. (www.backstage.com), the *Hollywood Reporter* (www.hollywoodreporter.com), and the monthly publication the *Ross Reports* (www.backstage.com/bso/rossreports/index.jsp). If you prefer not to purchase them there, go to www.dramabookshop.com —the online address of the Drama Bookshop in New York.

Once you've gotten an audition for a film or play, Showfax can provide sides for current auditions (www.showfax.com). The resource pages for actors on this site (the "Actor's Resource Portal") are chockfull of information that will help you learn about the business, from information on casting directors and trade publications to actor's websites and demo reels. Also offered are articles and columns designed to help you become a well-informed actor, along with discussion boards and other opportunities to learn. This is another great site you can visit to learn about the business aspect of an acting career.

Through Actors Access (www.actorsaccess.com), Showfax's partner site, you can scan casting notices placed by casting directors and some of the breakdowns (opportunities to submit photos/resumes) that are made public to actors. Even more options are available for union actors.

The Internet offers a vast array of resources. With a little care in watching out for yourself and your bank account, it can be an invaluable tool for the professional actor.

extra work and other jobs

A s you've learned, it can take a long time to become well known enough as an actor that you're auditioning for roles that pay a living wage. But there are other ways actors can get work to support themselves that are related to the acting business. This chapter will help you learn about extra work, print work, and industrial films.

EXTRA WORK

Extra work is a type of acting job, usually in film, where you are a background player. Most of the time, extra performers—or *extras*—don't have any lines but are simply seated at a table in a restaurant in which a scene takes place or walking down a street behind the lead performers as they do their scenes.

It's important to know about extra work, because it can be a good way to make money as an actor and to meet other people in the business. Some actors make most of their living from extra work. These actors are known as professional extras.

Extra work can also be a good way to get a foot in the door as an actor. Sometimes extras are "upgraded" on the day they do the work, which means they may be given some lines or some important action to do in a scene. This doesn't happen often, but a few actors have gotten their start as an extra by being upgraded in this way.

On soap operas, actors who play extra roles may be hired time after time, as doctors and nurses in the city's hospital, for instance. Sometimes they'll be given a few lines. If it's less than five lines, the job is called an *under-five*. If there are more lines, the actor becomes a *day player*. If the soap's casting person likes your work as an extra, he or she may call you to audition for a larger role. For this reason, extra work can be worth doing for any actor starting out. The next time you watch a movie or TV show, look for the extra performers in scenes that happen in public places. Notice how professionally they blend into the background.

One thing to be careful about if you choose to promote yourself for extra work is that some actors can get known by casting people as extra performers *only*. Then, when a role comes up that they might be right for, the casting person doesn't even think of them. In his or her mind, that actor is an extra performer. This usually only happens over a long period of time, after a casting person has called an actor again and again to be an extra.

If your choice is to make money as an actor however you can, or to be a professional extra, that's fine. But if you're doing extra work while hoping to do larger roles, be careful. This is a good example of getting carried along by whatever is happening in your career and not making your own choice about whether it's what you want to do. If you were being called for a lot of extra work, and you'd really rather have larger roles, you might think about turning some of the extra work down. You could say, "No, thank you, I'm already booked"—that way, casting people might not think of you only as an extra.

So, doing extra work can help you to make a living as an actor, but it needs to be your choice as to whether you want to do it.

PRINT WORK

Just as some actors are professional extras, some actors do *print* work to make money. Print work involves having photos of yourself taken for magazine ads and catalogues. It's the same type of work as modeling. You may have seen some faces over and over in ads. Most of the people in ads are professional models who are very attractive, but there is a market for people who have a more everyday look.

In magazine ads, you'll see all types of people, from young mothers caring for children to older people who take vitamins. To be successful in print work, you do need to be fairly attractive, and it helps if your looks fit into one of the types we have talked about. Spend some time looking at ads in magazines and see if you can figure out where you fit in. Do you look like the college kids in the jeans ads? Or do you look like the person who suffers from those pounding headaches? You can learn a lot about your type by studying the print work you see all around you. The closer you are to a type, the better your chances will be.

Print work is usually handled through agencies, just as acting work is. If you look in the guides that list people in the business, such as the *Ross Reports* (www.backstage.com/bso/rossreports/index.jsp), you'll find out which agencies handle print work. You'll need a photo and resume, just as you do as an actor, and you can contact the print agencies in the same way.

What's different about print work is that you're not actually *acting* on a **shoot**. You may play the role of a young parent or a businessperson, but you don't learn lines and blocking. The director will place you in certain positions to be photographed doing certain actions. But the shots will be still pictures, not movies or videotape, and this means not moving much, if at all.

> **Shoot:** This is slang for a photography session, as well as for the process of making a film.

In print work, it's very important that you dress exactly as if you are the type of person they're looking for. If you're going to an interview for a print job where they want a business person, your look and behavior must say, "I am a businessperson," right down to the way your hair is combed and your shoes are shined. There are so many actors who have a good look for print work that you need to present a very clear image.

Print work is also a good way actors make part of their living. But, again, you should do it because you want to, not just because it happened to come your way. If you don't enjoy it, then you should look into other ways to support yourself and to enjoy yourself as much as you can while you're making a living.

If you're serious about print work, you'll need to get a *composite photo* done. This is a photo that shows you as several different characters, such as a doctor, an executive, a mechanic—those character types you are right for. If you liked the photographer who did your headshots, call the same one to do your composite. He or she will probably be able to help you choose some characters for the shots and may even know where you can get a uniform or costume if you need one.

Any time you enjoy working with someone in the business—a photographer, makeup person, director, actor—keep that person on a list of people to stay in touch with. This is how you make your network grow. You never know when that person's skills will come in handy again. You may refer another actor to a fantastic makeup person, and that actor may later be able to help you meet an agent. You never know how your contacts will pan out in the future.

TALKING ABOUT ACTING

Is there anything you don't like about acting?

Xenia, age 14: *I don't like the uncertainty of acting as a career. People have to work from role to role, and that is a bit exciting, but what it really is, is scary.*

Yes, some people do see this as exciting. It's like gambling, in a way, because you're betting that you're talented or lucky enough to make it as an actor. It's normal to be scared by the risk. That's an important part of choosing whether to pursue a career. If you choose an acting career, you need to be sure it's what you want to do, even if you're scared. If you're not sure, it will probably be harder to do everything you need to do to succeed.

INDUSTRIAL FILMS

Industrial films are short films or videos made for businesses (industries and companies). These are films that promote a company's products or educate its employees or clients. For instance, IBM might make a video that is shown to new employees to tell them about some of the company's policies. Or a cleaning service might make a video that teaches their workers how to use cleaning products safely.

Industrial films offer a variety of work for actors. They are usually made in just a few days—they don't take weeks or months as a television film or movie would.

What you'll need if you want to do industrial films is much the same as what you need to do print work. You'll need photos and resumes, plus some film training. (If you already have composite shots for print work, you can use them to hunt down work in industrials.)

Pursuing extra work, print work, or work in industrial films is just another one of those choices actors make to earn money, and these are choices that you'll have to make again and again.

you can be what you want to be

Now you have a clear picture of what real life is like for an actor. Is an acting career what you really want for yourself? This is really the main question, and the reason you're reading this book.

Choosing what you want to do with your life is an important decision—one you should think about over a long period. Knowing what you're hoping to get out of an acting career can help you decide if it's really for you. Why do you want to be an actor? Think back to the first time you performed, whether it was at home in front of friends, or on a stage in front of an audience. You probably felt a big thrill, being up in front of people and having all their attention. And if there was applause, you experienced their enjoyment and appreciation for what you did.

Ask yourself what it was that you took away from that experience that made you think, "I'd like to do this over and over and over again!" Here are some of the reasons actors love acting:

"I love being able to pretend to be someone else, live in a different world."

—MADIGAN, age 15

"I like the fact that you can just leave reality and invent a new perspective."

—DANIEL, age 16

"I can be honest and express vivid emotions that I experience in my own life."

—PATRICK, age 16

"I like learning about my own emotional depth."

—ARIELLE, age 17

"People listen to you."

—MIKE, age 16

"It's always great to see how far you can stretch yourself."

—RYAN, age 16

"I like the different layers that can be explored."

—JOELLA, age 15

"I enjoy getting an emotional reaction out of the audience."

—JUSTINE, age 15

"I love making people feel something."

—ALISTAIR, age 17

"I enjoy the feeling of sending someone home from the theater in a good mood, or changed in some way."

—DANIEL, age 17

"I'm able to see things from others' point of view. Acting helps me understand human emotion and helps me be patient with people when they react in a different way."

—JULIANA, age 16

Think about what really draws you to acting, because that can be a key to understanding what you want out of your life and what would make you happy. Is an acting career the *only* thing you want, or are there other ways you'd be happy to live your life? If you choose acting as a career, would you feel like you're losing out on something else? Or would you feel like you lost out if you did *not* make a career of acting? Don't make up your mind right away, but give it careful thought. And know that the process of life means you can always change your mind and choose a different path. Let's talk about some of the issues you'll want to consider while you're deciding.

WHAT CHOICES MEAN

Choosing one thing often means accepting something you may not like that comes with it or giving up something else that you want.

We've already talked about how hard it can be to make your living as an actor. The stress that comes with it is an important issue to think about. If you simply want to be able to act, do different roles, and be in lots of shows, you can do that in community theater. In that case, you can get training for a different career in which you can make a living with less stress. Then you could do your acting in the evenings and on weekends. This could be a good way to do what you love without having to face the enormous competition of a professional career.

But if you really want a *professional* career in which you would also act in film and on television, then you'll need to accept the stress. You'll need to put most of your time and energy into achieving your goal. And that means giving up some other things.

Many actors have given up the possibility of getting married and having a family. They've chosen instead to devote themselves to their careers. There's nothing wrong with making this choice—for some it's just right. But when you're making your decision it's good to know about some of the things you may have to give up—at least for a while. It's not easy to keep a partnership going smoothly or to raise children when you've dedicated yourself to such a difficult profession. Acting can add to the difficulty with the need to move from job to job and travel often.

You might decide to work on your career for ten years and then ask, "Am I happy with my acting career?" Some actors do change their minds after a time and switch to another kind of work so they don't have to give up starting a family or other things they want to do with their lives.

EXCITEMENT AND FUN

Many young people see the way the lives of big movie stars are shown on TV and think it's a wonderful life. When an actor reaches a certain level of success, it can be wonderful. But some actors become sad or discouraged after trying over and over to get work for a long time. Their careers may not turn out as they had expected.

You might be looking for some excitement and fun in a career. But there is usually more than one way to find what you're looking for. As an actor, you'd be playing different roles, working with interesting people, having your picture taken, and maybe even performing in Hollywood movies. But if it takes fifteen or twenty years of very hard work and a single-minded focus for most actors to get there, it makes sense to try other ways to find excitement and fun if that's what you're primarily looking for. Think about what you've enjoyed doing in your life: do you love sports, or making music, or exploring new places? There are many things to explore in life, and many ways to have fun—and hardly any of them takes fifteen or twenty years.

Even if you do decide to become a professional actor, don't forget about all the other parts of life that can give you enjoyment.

Some actors like playing different roles and getting out of their ordinary lives to be someone else for a while. Most people have this wish, even non-actors. It's really just an urge to express yourself. There are many ways to do that besides being an actor. You can use your sense of humor in everyday life. You can go camping one weekend and dance the tango in a class the next. There are many ways to let all those different sides of yourself come out. And it's much easier to set up a camping trip or take a dance class (or whatever you enjoy) than it is to win success as an actor.

TALKING ABOUT ACTING

If you feel, as one young actor expressed, that you "can't live without acting," you may run into difficulty if your career doesn't turn out the way you expected. This young actor has made acting her life: she expects it to keep her going, to take care of her needs, to feed her emotionally, intellectually, and spiritually—and that is a very difficult aim to achieve in any career, let alone a career with incredibly stiff competition and extremely uncertain employment statistics.

WHAT DO YOU REALLY WANT?

Do you really want to be an actor, or could it be that you simply want to be able to express your feelings? Or to explore some of the infinite possibilities in life? One reason some people choose to become actors is that it gives them a chance to do that.

For most of our country's history, feelings were something people kept quiet about. Today our society is more comfortable with letting people express their feelings. It's normal to have strong feelings that you want to express, such as sadness or anger or fear. It's simply part of being human.

Some people are still not comfortable allowing others to express their feelings. Some families are set in their ways and don't encourage family members to try new things or explore life. This may be true in your family. That could lead you to believe that the only way you can express yourself or try new things is through acting, because acting offers the opportunity to try on new roles, experience new situations, and be someone different. But this does not have to lead you to choose acting as a career. Acting is certainly not the only way to discover new experiences or express your feelings.

As you get older, you'll make friends who may understand you better than your family does. You can learn to express more of your feelings and more of yourself, and you can explore life to your heart's content. When you're an adult, you can make all kinds of different choices about who you want to be and how you want to live your life. You'll no longer have to live totally by the rules set up in your family.

So this matter of feelings can affect your choice about becoming a professional actor—or not. As an adult you'll have lots of chances to let out all the things that are deep within you, even feelings that seem trapped inside. Think about what it is that really draws you to acting, what you're truthfully hoping to achieve. Then you'll see whether you really want to be an actor or simply to want be free to express yourself, explore, and pursue your own interests.

This idea may take you some time to comprehend. If you're confused about feelings or family situations, you might ask a teacher or school career counselor to help you understand. The important thing to remember is that you can find ways to be happy no matter what you decide to do with your life.

MAKE YOUR OWN DECISION

It's also important for you to make the decision yourself. When you choose a career, you should choose it because it's something *you* want to do. Sometimes parents push kids into certain careers. For instance, your family might want you to be a doctor so you'll be able to help people and make a good living—and you might even get the feeling that if you were a doctor, your parents would be especially proud. But you probably won't be happy with a career based on what someone else wants. The world is full of people who followed someone else's wishes about what to do with their lives. After time goes by, they're sad or angry that they were pushed into it, and they're not happy with their lives. Then it takes a lot of work to make a change.

TALKING ABOUT ACTING

Is there any advice you'd give to young actors?

Yvette, age 21: *Just do it and have fun, and don't get to caught up in it. Because you can do whatever you want with your life.*

It's okay to accept advice and think about ideas that other people have to give you. But do what you want with your life. Don't let anyone talk you into something you're not sure about. Your life is yours to spend the way you choose. Make your decision with care, and pay attention to your feelings, to what you want, as you go along. Pursue the things that make you happy, and you'll be more successful, no matter what you choose.

If you're set on being a professional actor, then go for it! Focus your heart, your mind, and your spirit on what you want! I'll be applauding for you.

zeroing in on books

Actors are always reading. Books are great sources of information that can help them with their careers. And books give them inspiration to grow and improve as artists.

Here are some books on a number of topics that I would suggest you take a look at. I have marked with a star (*) the ones that are especially good for younger actors.

ACTING SKILLS

Barr, Tony. *Acting for the Camera: Revised Edition*. Harper Paperbacks, 1997.

Bates, Brian. The *Way of the Actor: A Path to Knowledge & Power*. Shambhala, 2001.

*Boleslavsky, Richard. *Acting: The First Six Lessons*. Routledge, 1987.

*Brebner, Ann. *Setting Free the Actor: Overcoming Creative Blocks*. Mercury House, 1990.

Caine, Michael. *Acting in Film*. Applause, 2000.

Chaikin, Joseph. *The Presence of the Actor*. Theatre Communications, 1991.

Cole, Toby & Helen K. Chinoy. *Actors on Acting*. Three Rivers Press, 1995.

Hagen, Uta & Haskel Frankel. *Respect for Acting*. Wiley, 1973.

Olivier, Laurence. *On Acting*. Simon & Schuster, 1987.

Stanislavski, Constantin. *An Actor Prepares*. Theatre Arts Books, 1989.

Stanislavski, Constantin. *Building a Character*. Theatre Arts Books, 1989.

Stanislavski, Constantin. *Creating a Role*. Theatre Arts Books, 1989.

AUDITIONING

Harmon, Renee. *How to Audition for Movies & TV.* Walker & Co., 1992.

Hooks, Ed. *The Audition Book.* Back Stage Books, 2000.

Hunt, Gordon. *How to Audition: For TV, Movies, Commercials, Plays, and Musicals.* Collins, 1995.

Oliver, Donald. *How to Audition for the Musical Theatre.* Smith & Kraus, 1995.

See, Joan. *Acting in Commercials: A Guide to Auditioning and Performing on Camera.* Back Stage Books, 2007.

Shurtleff, Michael. *Audition: Everything an Actor Needs to Know to Get the Part.* Bantam, 1980.

Silver, Fred. *Auditioning for the Musical Theatre.* Penguin, 1988.

Tucker, Patrick. *Secrets of Screen Acting.* Theatre Arts Books, 2003.

THE BUSINESS OF ACTING

Adams, Brian. *Screen Acting: How to Succeed in Motion Pictures.* Lone Eagle Publishing, 1987.

Buzzell, Linda. *How to Make It in Hollywood.* Collins, 1996.

*Callan, K. *How to Sell Yourself as an Actor.* Sweden Press, 2002.

Charles, Jill, and Tom Bloom. *The Actor's Picture/Resume Book.* Theatre Directories, 1998.

Clark, Elaine. *There's Money Where Your Mouth Is: An Insider's Guide to a Career in Voice-Overs.* Back Stage Books, 2000.

Fridell, Squire. *Acting in Television Commercials for Fun & Profit.* Three Rivers Press, 1995.

Henry, Mari Lyn, and Lynne Rogers. *How to Be a Working Actor.* Back Stage Books, 2000.

*Hurtes, Hettie Lynne. *The Back Stage Guide to Casting Directors: Who They Are, How They Work, What They Look for in Actors.* Back Stage Books, 1998.

Lewis, M. K. & Rosemary R. Lewis. *Your Film Acting Career: How to Break into the Movies & TV & Survive in Hollywood.* Gotham House, 1997.

Logan, Tom, and Marvin Paige. *How to Act & Eat at the Same Time: The Business of Landing a Professional Acting Job.* Communications Press, 1988.

Mayfield, Katherine. *Smart Actors, Foolish Choices: A Self-Help Guide to Coping with the Emotional Stresses of the Business.* Back Stage Books, 1996.

O'Neil, Brian. *Acting as a Business: Strategies for Success.* Heinemann, 2005.

Searle, Joan. *Getting the Part. Thirty-Three Professional Casting Directors Tell You How to Get Work in Theater, Films, Commercials, & TV.* Limelight Editions, 2004.

*Small, Edgar. *From Agent to Actor: An Unsentimental Education or What the Other Half Knows.* Samuel French, 1991.

Theatre Communications Guild, ed. *Theatre Directory 2005-06.* TCG, 2005.

Tumielewicz, P.J. and Peg Lyons, editors. *Directory of Theatre Training Programs 2005–2007*. Dorset Theatre Festival, 2006.

Tumielewicz, P.J. and Barbara Ax, editors. *Regional Theatre Directory*. Theatre Directories, 2006.

Tumielewicz, P.J. and Peg Lyons, editors. *Summer Theatre Directory*. Theatre Directories, 2006.

OTHER HELPFUL BOOKS

Armstrong, Thomas. *Seven Kinds of Smart*. Plume, 1999.

Bramson, Robert M. *Coping with Difficult People*. Dell, 1988.

Cameron, Julia. The *Artist's Way*. Tarcher, 2002.

Grabhorn, Lynn. *Excuse Me, Your Life is Waiting: The Astonishing Power of Feelings*. Hampton Roads Publishing, 2003.

James, Muriel, and John James. *Passion for Life*. Dutton, 1991.

Kabat-Zinn, Jon. *Wherever You Go, There You Are*. Hyperion, 2005.

Laut, Phil. *Money Is My Friend*. Ballantine Books, 1999.

Lehmkul, Dorothy, and Dolores Cotter Lamping. *Organizing for the Creative Person*. Crown, 1993.

Lieberman, Annette, and Vicki Lindner. *Unbalanced Accounts: How Women Can Overcome Their Fear of Money*. Viking Penguin, 1987.

Maisel, Eric. *Staying Sane in the Arts*. Putnam, 1992.

*Miller, Alice. *The Drama of the Gifted Child*. Basic Books, 1996.

Miller, Alice. *Thou Shalt Not Be Aware*. Farrar, Straus & Giroux, 1998.

Newman, Mildred, and Bernard Berkowitz. *How to Be Your Own Best Friend*. Ballantine Books, 1986.

Winter, Barbara J. *Making a Living Without a Job*. Bantam, 1993.

glossary

Ad lib: Making up a line or lines on the spot. When an actor forgets a line, or is supposed to make an entrance and doesn't, the other actors can lose their place or have no way to continue the action if they do not invent dialogue or action. This is called ad-libbing.

Blocking: Movement patterns given to the actors by the director to set up a specific "picture" that helps the audience understand the scene.

Business Class: A business class can teach you how to organize your career as a business and help you set up a self-promotion plan so that you're clear on the tasks needed to get work as an actor.

Callback: This term is used a great deal by actors. It means a second audition or interview for the same role. You usually audition in front of more people at the callback than you do at the first audition.

Casting director: This person's job is to stay abreast of the talent pool of actors and to arrange for actors who are right for a role to audition for a director or producer in the process of casting a play, commercial, or film.

Character actor: An actor who is known for creating unusual and interesting characters. What great character actors in today's films spring to mind for you?

Characterization: Preparing to act a role by deciding how a character looks, behaves, sounds, thinks, feels—and so on. Characterization is a very complex process which is generally taught in acting training programs.

Cold reading: Reading aloud a scene from the script without rehearsing, to see how you would fit with a role.

Cover letter: A letter that introduces you and states the reason you're contacting the person. People in most careers send cover letters with their resumes when they inquire about a job. You'll need to send a cover letter when you mail your photo and resume to a casting director or agent. (See page 130 for an example.)

Credits: The list on your resume of the roles you've played. Also refers to actors listed in a film—i.e., the opening credits or the credits which run at the end of a film.

Curtain time: The time the show begins. This term is used whether there's a curtain in the theater or not.

Fencing: In the historic past, gentlemen fought in wars or settled arguments by dueling with swords, or fencing. Some of Shakespeare's plays, such as *Hamlet*, include scenes in which the actors fence. In the last few decades, fencing has become popular as a sport in itself.

Flyers: These are announcements, usually printed on one sheet of colored paper, of the performances of a play, the location of the theater, the dates and times of the show, and the cast. They are simple tools for promoting shows and the actors in them.

General audition: An audition usually conducted at an actors' union office, such as

Actor's Equity. These auditions are sometimes held by a repertory company before they cast the next season of plays so that they can meet new actors. Some of the major roles in their productions may be cast before these auditions are held, but the directors are often looking for actors to fill supporting and smaller roles.

General interview: An "interview" with someone in the business with the primary purpose of simply meeting, not usually for a particular role or project. An agent or casting director may call an actor in for a general interview if he or she is impressed with the actor's work or promotion package to meet the actor in person.

Green room: The traditional name for the room where actors wait before and between their time onstage. According to *Wikipedia*, the most widely accepted origin of the term dates back to Shakespearean times, when actors prepared for their performances in a room filled with plants and shrubs because it was believed that the moisture in the topiary was beneficial to the actors' voices.

Headshot: An actor's headshot is an 8-by-10 black-and-white photo that normally includes his or her head and shoulders. In recent years, "three-quarter" photos have become common. These show the actor's face and body down to about the hips or knees. The headshot is usually 10 inches high and 8 inches wide (portrait style), but some actors prefer to get prints that are 8 inches high and 10 inches wide.

Improvisation: In an improvisation (or *improv*), two or more actors act out a short scene without knowing how it will go. They are given a theme or situation to begin, and they make up the words and actions as they go along. Improvisation helps actors learn to be creative.

Look: Many casting directors and agents tend to put actors into groups based on their appearance. This leads to a practice known as *typecasting*. As the term suggests, what *type* an actor appears to be is part of what lands him or her the job. The young mom, the doctor, the tough guy—these are familiar types that actors play again and again—if they have a certain look.

Mailing list: When you start out as an actor, figure out a way to keep track of the people you meet and send photos to. Your mailing list should include everyone in the business you've had contact with (see chapter N, "Networking").

Monologue: A one- or two-minute speech by a character in a play or film that is not interrupted by other characters' lines.

Motivation: The reason the character performs the actions he or she does in the script.

Objective: What the character most wants in a scene, or in the play or film—the goal of the character's actions. An actor usually comes up with a character objective for each scene and a larger objective for the entire play. Some examples are trying to convince another character that your point of view is the right one, persuading another character to do something for yours, or asking for help with a problem. You should work toward your objective as the character with all the energy you can muster, with "every fiber of your being."

Postcard: A postcard-size marketing tool that usually includes one or two of your headshots (reduced) and your name and contact information. They cost much less to duplicate and mail than 8-by-10 headshots and help actors to keep in touch in a simple way.

Project: As an actor you must be able to throw—or project—the sound of your voice so that you are heard even in the back rows of the theater. It doesn't simply mean that you speak louder, although that is part of the skill. Projecting does not mean yelling. It's more like taking the energy you use to speak during a conversation and magnifying it ten times to fill the space in a theater.

Promote: This term refers to the tasks actors do to increase the chances that they'll get jobs on the stage, in films, and on TV. When a business begins to sell a product, it usually promotes it through marketing and advertising. When you promote yourself as an actor, you're advertising yourself as a professional, ready to do a role.

Regional Theater: Refers to professional theaters anwhere in the country outside of New York City.

Repertory: At repertory theaters, several shows are chosen for the season. The actors rehearse the first show and then begin performing it in the evenings while they rehearse the second show during the day. Then the second show will be added to the evening performances. Rehearsals for the third show then begin during the day. There are plenty of stories about repertory theater actors who put on the wrong costume for the play that night, so if you find yourself working in rep, you'll want to be careful to keep track of the shows.

Scene study: In this type of acting class, the teacher asks you to pick a scene from a play or assigns you a scene and helps you and a partner work on it. Then, any work you do on your acting technique is done when it's needed in that scene.

Sense memory: When you recall an experience you stored in your memory and use it in your acting, you are using your sense memory. For example, in some scenes you may need to act being cold. Your senses have been affected by cold in the past, so you begin reacting the same way—by shivering or rubbing your hands. Actors' performances are more realistic when they use their past sensations as tools in this way.

Shoot: This is slang for a photography session, as well as for the process of making a film.

Sides: The parts of the script you'll be auditioning with. Most often, they include the entire scene but occasionally will only include the actor's cue followed by the lines.

Soaps: Soap operas are often called soaps, for short. Both terms refer to daytime television dramas. The term "soap opera" first came about because manufacturers advertised laundry soap during the commercials.

Subtext: The silent "monologue" an actor creates for his or her character, which includes thoughts, wishes, and statements of feeling. We all have a "subtext" running through our minds most of the time, and creating an interesting subtext can produce a fascinating character, because the audience wants to know what's going on in the character's head.

Take: A single scene in a film, commercial, or TV show, shot from beginning to end, is a take. When everything is ready for the shot, the stage manager holds a clapboard in front of the camera. On it is written the number of the take. He or she will say, "Take One" (or "Take Two" for the second filming of the scene, and so on), and snap shut the clapboard. The clap it makes as it is shut helps the editor match up the image on the film with the sounds on the soundtrack.

Temporary agency: A "temp" business has a number of client companies and hires you for only a day, a week, or a month to work at one of those companies.

Trades: The nickname given to theater publications such as *Hollywood Reporter*, *Variety*, and *BackStage*.

Vocal range: This refers to the type of voice you have: bass, baritone, tenor, alto, mezzo-soprano, or soprano. You can find out from a voice teacher, vocal coach, or choir director what type of voice you have if you don't know offhand. Provide your range on your resume only if you sing very well—casting directors may call you to audition for singing roles.

Warm up: This is the process of exercising your body and voice so that you're relaxed and energetic when you get onstage.

helpful websites

www.abcpictures.com – photo reproduction services from ABC Pictures in Missouri, which has been supplying actors with photos and postcards for years.

www.actormail.com – ActorMail provides business and mailing services for professional actors.

www.actorsaccess.com – This is the actors' site for the Breakdown Services, which provide sides for professional auditions.

www.actorsfund.org – a site that offers crisis counseling for actors, along with some financial aid and other programs specifically for actors.

www.backstage.com – *Back Stage* and *Back Stage West*, the weekly theater newspapers in New York and L.A.

www.backstage.com/bso/rossreports/index.jsp – website for the *Ross Reports*, the monthly listing of who's who in casting and agenting.

www.dramabookshop.com – the online address of the Drama Bookshop in New York.

www.hendersonenterprises.com – This company provides preprinted address labels for casting directors, agents, personal managers, theater companies, and more, as well as guides to people in the business (under Books/Publications) and books for actors. Visit this site to get a feel for what the business aspect of show business is all about. Label sets are not overly expensive and can save lots of time—instead of typing addresses on your own labels, just add a pre-printed one to address your envelope.

www.hollywoodreporter.com – The *Hollywood Reporter*

www.magnet.edu – Many Magnet high schools have excellent performing arts programs. Competition can be very strong, but you can begin your acting training earlier than you would at a college or university.

http://nast.arts-accredit.org/ – A list of accredited theater schools belonging to the National Association of Schools of Theater.

www.nfaa.org – the National Foundation for Advancement in the Arts, which administers the Arts Recognition and Talent Search for high school students.

www.showfax.com – Showfax provides sides for professional auditions. The site is also full of useful information for actors.

www.stagedoormanor.com – Stage Door Manor is a professionally oriented summer theater camp in Loch Sheldrake, NY.

www.urta.com – The University/Resident Theatre Association holds auditions for master's degree programs in connection with resident theater companies.

www.variety.com – *Variety*

www.waldentheatre.org – The Walden Theatre in Louisville, KY, offers professional conservatory-style classes and summer camp sessions.

index